WHOLEHEAR

Beth Hallinan was born in 1939 in County Cork, Ireland, and brought up in the West Indies, where her father was with the Colonial Service. She studied at the Guildhall School of Music and Drama and later taught history and English at the Westminster Cathedral Choir School. Her family then moved to Southampton, where she started cooking directors' lunches, specialising in banks, 'like Bonnie and Clyde'.

Her first book, *Cooking For Your Heart's Sake*, was published by Hamlyn in 1978. It was one of the first books in this country on low-cholesterol food and was one of the top twelve bestselling cookbooks of the year. Her second book, *Cooking with Yogurt*, was published the following year. Both books have gone into several editions and into paperback, and are still in print.

Beth opened her first restaurant in Hamble in 1979, as chef patron. *Beth's* found its way into the *Guide Michelin*, *The Good Food Guide* and *Egon Ronay* and, more importantly, into the hearts of a large number of local customers and visiting yachtsmen.

Now living in London, in addition to acting as a restaurant consultant Beth has contributed regular cookery pieces to two Irish newspapers, the *Sunday Independent* and the *Cork Examiner*.

'We must educate people away from the dangerous idea that you can control heart disease by not eating foods such as eggs, butter and milk'

Dr Linus Pauling, winner of two Nobel prizes.

WHOLEHEARTED COOKING

the complete
LOW-CHOLESTEROL
cookbook

Beth Hallinan

ARROW BOOKS

Arrow Books Limited
20 Vauxhall Bridge Road, London SW1V 2SA

An imprint of Random Century Group

London Melbourne Sydney Auckland Johannesburg
and agencies throughout the world

First published in 1991

© Beth Hallinan 1991

Illustrations by Leslie Dean

Phototypeset by Intype, London
Printed and bound in Great Britain by
Cox & Wyman Ltd, Reading

ISBN 0 09 971370 5

CONTENTS

ACKNOWLEDGEMENTS

I would like to thank the following people who gave their kind permission for their recipes to be included in this book.

My dear friend Angela Kirby supplied the recipe for *Grandmother's Braised Steak* – a recipe passed down to her by her grandmother.

The recipe for *Porc à l'Orange* is based on a recipe given to me years ago by another kind and talented friend, Mrs Joan Hill.

The recipes for *Carrageen Moss Pudding* and *Ballymaloe Brown Bread* come from a very generous and famous cook, Myrtle Allen of Ballymaloe House, County Cork.

Finally, the recipe for *Boston Baked Beans* is adapted from *The Boston Cooking School Cookbook*.

One

INTRODUCTION

'Thank God there is no cholesterol in women. At least He got something right,' grumbles Mel Calman. 'What He was doing putting cholesterol into ice cream and chocolate, I'll never know. He should have put it into something boring like coal dust.' Amen to that: it pretty well sums up what we all think.

We have the most wonderful foodstuffs in the world, with an abundance of meat, fish, game, vegetables, salads, fruits, breads, pulses, cereals and nuts – readily available all the year round. We are spoilt for choice and unsurpassable quality, but it is an unavoidable fact that here in Britain we now claim the doubtful distinction of having one of the highest incidences of heart disease in the world. Coronary disease kills more than 150,000 people in England and Wales every year. Over 20,000 of these are aged under 60, and significant numbers are under 45.

We have for many centuries been a dairy-producing country, and so this alone cannot explain the increase in deaths from heart disease. It is true that we have long been enjoying a diet that is rich in fats, but our dietary habits and patterns have changed in another way. Because we are not so physically active as we were thirty years ago, we are eating *less*. Not less fats, though – rather more; but less carbohydrates. So the balance between fat and starchy food in our diet has gone wrong.

This is the age of 'snacking' on chips, crisps and convenience foods, which tend to be deep-fried and laden with saturated fats. McDonald's and Kentucky Fried Chicken have crossed the Atlantic to join the fish-and-chip shops and the Chinese take-aways – more fatty foods, unwholesome but quick and filling. The ingredients seem to be addictive, and the emotive forces of the packing and promotion have turned them into cult food.

What we need is a *better* way of eating, avoiding harmful fats and including more fibre.

It is immensely important to start our children on good eating habits from tiny babies. These good habits will be with them for life. Young children have to be protected, to an extent, from the forces of advertising and big business. A taste for good food has to come from their parents, and be conveyed in a simple and irresistible way.

The principles of cooking for a healthy heart are really easy, even for the most inexperienced cook. The benefits are obvious – not just to the heart, but to general fitness, figure, appearance and vitality.

THE HEART

'You gotta have heart', says the song – somewhat unnecessarily. What is also incontestably true is that we only have one heart and so we had better take great care of it.

Inherited genes determine the equipment you are born with; your lifestyle decides the rest. Our family history, age and sex are beyond our control – although awareness of inherited tendencies can lead to early detection of a heart problem.

These are the factors you *can* control:

smoking
high blood pressure
diet
obesity
stress

Smoking is an addiction which can be hugely difficult to kick, but it can and must be done by those who do not want to throw away their health and their life. High blood pressure is aggravated by smoking, so smoking compounds that problem too. High blood pressure (like heart disease) is not always apparent. Not experiencing any symptoms can lull one into a false sense of security. 'No news is good news' is not the truth here, and that is why it is important to check the blood pressure regularly. Blood pressure goes up and down naturally. It's when it stays up that it causes troubles that can lead to heart attack and strokes. So everyone over the age of 25 should have the simple test (done by a nurse or doctor) at least every five years.

A moderate and healthy lifestyle is the key to preventing high blood pressure. Cut down or, better still, cut out smoking. Take enough regular exercise and fresh air, and control your weight.

Overweight and over-high cholesterol levels should not be confused. A skinny person can have over-high cholesterol levels. However, being overweight can lead to coronary heart disease (CHD) because of the added burden on the heart. (Imagine always having to carry a basket of shopping.) This book is not about losing weight, but anyone who follows a balanced diet will automatically find their correct weight level.

All research, including the most recent studies, has shown the value of diet in the prevention of coronary disease. A reduced intake of fats – especially saturated fats – sugar and salt together with an increased intake of fibre-rich foods is vital to reducing the likelihood of heart disease.

CORONARY HEART DISEASE

The heart is a muscle, about the size of a clenched fist, that pumps blood around the body through arteries. It contracts about seventy times every minute. At birth the arteries are lined with a smooth tissue, which by its nature helps the blood to flow freely. Minute cracks start to develop with the constant flexing and twisting each time the heart contracts and relaxes. 'Patches' of fat and cholesterol rush to repair the damage. When the blood has too high a level of cholesterol, the particles are too large to be absorbed through the artery wall. There is a rapid build-up of fatty deposits and new cells developing to absorb them. The accumulation of these new cholesterol-filled cells gradually narrows the arteries, and the heart has to pump harder to do its work. This blockage and build-up of plaque (arteriosclerosis) can eventually stop the blood supply altogether. This is coronary heart disease (CHD) and has two main forms: angina and heart attack. Many people are quite unaware that they suffer from CHD until they have a heart attack.

WHAT IS ANGINA?

If the arteries are blocked with atheroma (plaque), the heart is unable to get the oxygen it needs to cope with an increased call, such as extra strain from exercise. This gives a feeling of heavy, cramp-like pain, like a great weight across the chest. This pain eases as the sufferer rests and the heart's workload returns to normal. This pain is called *angina*. The pain of angina can be lessened by drugs or surgery. People who suffer from angina are more likely to suffer heart attack.

WHAT IS HEART ATTACK?

Heart attack happens when a coronary artery becomes blocked and the blood supply to the heart that is fed by that artery stops. If a large part of the artery is blocked, a large part of the heart muscle will be badly affected, sometimes causing the heart to stop beating altogether.

A person who suffers a heart attack will experience symptoms which vary from such minor discomforts that he or she may not even report them to the doctor. (It is, however, a great mistake to overlook even the mildest warning of CHD.) More commonly, however, the person suffers very severe chest pain, may faint, sweats and feels sick and giddy. In cases where the heart stops beating, the person will quickly die unless resuscitated immediately. It is important not to lose sight of the fact that angina and heart attack are the results of *arteriosclerosis*, the build-up of plaque in the arteries.

PREVENTION IS BETTER THAN CURE

Much effort, time and money have gone into medical research on heart attack, and countless people have had to be helped to cope with the crippling effects of heart disease. But we, as individuals, can so easily learn to exercise control over the development of over-high levels of fats in our blood which can lead to CHD.

Without preventive measures, the incidence of CHD continues to increase, but it is possible to do something about it. This has already been demonstrated in the United States of America, which has achieved a significant reduction in CHD in the last few years. The improvement in Britain has so far only been very slight.

A lot has been learned about blood fats and the effects of diet on the heart and it's not all negative. A diet for a healthy heart restricts the intake of harmful fats, but – even more importantly – *metabolises* them correctly. The results are increased energy, correct weight and sparkling health.

GETTING YOUR FATS STRAIGHT

We need fat in the diet because it has many functions and provides us with certain essentials. It is a source of energy, the most concentrated of all. Every gram of fat, of whatever sort, provides 9 calories or 37 kilojoules, i.e. more than twice the amount from carbohydrates (sugar and starch) or protein. Our Western-style diet is certainly too high in fat. Fat represents a staggering 40–50% of our calorie intake. Ideally we should reduce our consumption of *all* fats to 30%.

Most foods contain fat, so there is no *need* to add extra oils, cheese, butter and animal fats to a good diet that includes vegetables, fruits, nuts and grains in order to be healthy. The body can make its own fatty acids from the food eaten on a low-fat and low-protein diet (one exception to this is linoleic acid, which the body cannot make but which can be got from salad oils – excepting olive oil – and nuts, especially walnuts).

There are three kinds of fats – saturated, polyunsaturated, and monounsaturated. All foods with fats contain some of each, but mainly one of them, e.g. sunflower oil is high in polyunsaturates.

Saturated fats: These are found in animal food products and in coconut and palm oil. A diet with a lot of saturated fats certainly leads to a higher cholesterol level in the blood and in turn to arteriosclerosis. So saturated fats should be kept to a minimum. It is, however, a mistake simply to replace them with polyunsaturated fats.

Polyunsaturated fats: These are found in vegetables, nuts, seeds and some fish. They do not raise cholesterol levels, and can even positively lower them (especially when consumed with monounsaturates). In spite of this apparent benefit I do not recommend you increase them too much as, like all fats, they are high in calories. Most importantly, these fats are very 'unstable', particularly at high temperatures such as they are subjected to in frying and baking. The particles can oxidise and break down to produce what are called free radicals. These form toxic peroxides which can destroy cells. This can lead to disease and premature ageing. Vitamin E helps to prevent damage from free radicals because it is an antioxidant. A diet that is high in polyunsaturates needs the help of extra vitamin E.

Monounsaturated fats: Monounsaturates have the advantage of being more stable at high cooking temperatures and can help to lower cholesterol levels. Olives and avocados are high in monounsaturates.

In short, saturated fats should be reduced or avoided altogether in a cholesterol-lowering plan, but moderate amounts of poly-unsaturates and monounsaturates may actually help to lower cholesterol. An increase in the consumption of carbohydrates like potatoes and porridge and wholemeal bread will provide the energy (calories) we need and *replace* some of the fatty calories which have been cut back. The total calorie intake will be much lower and this new balance of reduced fats and increased fibre will have hugely beneficial results on the heart and the body generally.

A FEW FACTS ABOUT BLOOD CHOLESTEROL

Pure cholesterol is an odourless, white powdery substance. You cannot taste it or see it in the foods you eat. Even if you did not eat foods with cholesterol the body would manufacture enough for its own needs.

This is because we need cholesterol to live. The body uses it to make essential cell walls as well as for various other functions. A normal component of body tissues, especialy those of the brain, nervous system, and liver, cholesterol acts as a lubricant for the arteries and is used to make adrenal and sex hormones, vitamin D, and bile, which digests fats. If the body is deprived altogether of cholesterol, *it will immediately compensate by producing more itself.*

Gall stones and deposits that build up on the artery walls in arteriosclerosis contain cholesterol, and for some years people assumed these problems were caused by high-cholesterol diets. But there is considerable evidence now to show that a failure to metabolise cholesterol is the real culprit. Too high an intake of cholesterol could certainly contribute towards these problems but does not necessarily cause them.

Cholesterol is like a fat in that it will not mix with water, so to carry it in the blood the body wraps it in protein 'packages'. The combination of cholesterol and protein is called lipoprotein. Not all lipoproteins are the same, and to distinguish them from each other they are described by their density: high density lipoproteins and low density lipoproteins, or HDL and LDL for short. The low density lipoproteins contain the greater percent-age of cholesterol and may be responsible for depositing chol-sterol on the artery walls. However, people with higher levels of HDLs (women in general, especially before the menopause) are less prone to heart disease. So the HDLs are the good guys and LDLs are the bad guys.

It is with lowering cholesterol in the blood that this book is concerned. A recently completed study showed that people who do have elevated blood cholesterol and who take steps to reduce it also reduce their risk of heart attack and CHD. Blood screening is now recognised as the most effective way of detecting heart disease. It is particularly important for people with a family history of heart trouble to have this test as they may have inherited tendencies to CHD. However, as CHD is the major cause of death in Great Britain, it is wise for everyone, both men and women, to be checked periodically. So, know your cholesterol level and make any necessary changes to your diet if your tests show over-high levels.

In short, cholesterol can be reduced and HDL levels increased if you:

- Know your cholesterol level, and maintain it at the right level.
- Enjoy a varied diet, high in fibre and low in fats.
- Take simple vitamin supplements, especially vitamin E and the B vitamins.
- Keep your weight within the recommended range for your age and height.
- Exercise regularly – this promotes a healthy heart and reduces stress.

Following these simple steps may avert the need for drug therapy later.

THE WAY TO LOWER CHOLESTEROL IN THE BLOOD

Modern diets rightly recommend those with an over-high cholesterol level to reduce their intake of saturated fats. They suggest that fish, poultry and game should replace fattier meats such as pork, lamb and beef. They also suggest increasing polyunsaturated oils in the diet. This is sound advice (especially when they are combined with monounsaturated olive oil), but *only when taken with enough vitamin E*. Without increasing vitamin E the result can lead to a heart attack.

Our modern diet often lacks vitamin E – for example it is discarded when flour is refined and when oil is chemically extracted. This is another instance of the need to choose unrefined foods – in this case wholemeal bread and cold-pressed oils. A few of the foods in which vitamin E is found are lettuce, parsley, spinach, mustard leaves, potatoes, leeks, carrots, cucumber, brown rice and honey.

It is not yet fully recognised that drastically reducing the intake of saturated fats alone could actually encourage the metabolism to produce even more cholesterol to compensate for the imposed reduction. The metabolism needs the added help of fibre- and vitamin-rich foods, together with plenty of exercise, to prevent it from going into 'overdrive' and producing even higher cholesterol levels.

The body's key to coping with cholesterol is lecithin. This is an emulsifier that works rather like washing-up liquid in a sink of dirty dishes; it breaks the fat up into smaller particles and disperses it. Lecithin helps cholesterol to pass efficiently through the arteries to do its essential work. Without it the particles of cholesterol are too large to pass through, so the level of cholesterol rises and some of it becomes lodged in the arterial walls, causing arteriosclerosis. Circulation becomes impaired as there is less and less room for the blood to flow through, and greater effort has to be exerted by the heart. Sufferers from heart disease characteristically show an increase in blood cholesterol *and a drop in lecithin*, so it is obviously vital to supplement the diet with additional lecithin.

Lecithin granules are easily obtainable and are not difficult to use (capsules do not supply a large enough quantity). The results will be very beneficial and greatly help to lower blood cholesterol. Two tablespoons of lecithin taken daily will reduce cholesterol in the blood by breaking the fats down so that they can be absorbed through the arterial wall and utilised by the tissues. Lecithin also increases the bile acids, which in turn decrease blood cholesterol.

The B vitamins choline, inositol and vitamin B6 are lost, as is the vitamin E, when flour is refined. Eighty-five per cent of B6 content is lost in this way. This is one of the reasons for the massive increase in heart disease in the so-called 'civilised' countries of the West since the early part of this century.

The body cannot produce enough lecithin without adequate choline and inositol. A deficiency in these will prevent the body from burning and excreting fats. Blood cholesterol will rise. In fact blood cholesterol can be reduced by choline and inositol alone. Liver, wheat germ and yeast are rich sources, and in addition a B complex supplement can be taken.

While it is obviously a help to limit the intake of saturated fats and increase the polyunsaturates, it is the greatest mistake to throw out the baby with the bath water and disallow many highly valuable and nutritious foods because they contain cholesterol. Valuable foods such as liver, brains and shellfish are usually struck off the list, although they themselves supply the nutrients for reducing cholesterol. This principle is carried even further by denying altogether foods like milk and butter, which actually benefit the heart. These foods should be *reduced* but by no means excluded for ever.

Butter is a fine natural product which is very good for you. *Too much* butter (like too much of anything) is not, and those who are on a cholesterol-lowering diet should restrict the intake of butter along with all other animal fats. Some margarines are made from vegetables which are high in polyunsaturates, but there are also cheaper brands which are made from unspecified oils and which may be higher in saturated fats than is butter. So look for the brands which are high in polyunsaturates. Margarine is not an entirely natural product, it also contains preservatives, flavourings, emulsifiers, stabilisers and colourings. There is no doubt in my mind that butter is far superior in taste and a good way to keep a balance is to do as the French do – restrict the use of butter to cooking, and spread polyunsaturated margarine on to bread or toast.

In recent times eggs have been maligned, because of the cholesterol in them, but they are an excellent source of protein. It is wrong to exclude them altogether, because they also contain lecithin, the natural emulsifier. (Lecithin, however, is destroyed by the high cooking temperatures of frying, and eggs should be poached, scrambled or boiled rather than fried.) As well as containing cholesterol and lecithin, eggs are a rich source of nutritional goodness. They provide sulphur, zinc, iron and phosphorus, and valuable fatty acids. Vitamins A, B2, D and E are present in good quantities. They do much to protect health and beauty, and even ward off ageing processes with the sulphur amino acids cystine and methionine.

A FEW SIMPLE GUIDELINES

- Avoid saturated fats. A simple approach is to switch straight away from cooking with solid fats. Never use animal fats for cooking again, but instead olive oil, which tolerates higher temperatures better than the polyunsaturated oils. Dress salads with sunflower or olive oil. Choose margarines that say 'high in polyunsaturates' on the label.
- Cut and discard fat from all meat and poultry. Avoid meats that are heavily marbled with fat.
- Skip sausage, bacon, salami and luncheon meat – all full of saturated fat.
- Roast meat on a rack so that the fat can be easily tipped away.
- Skim broths and stews of all fat (easiest done when cold) before serving.
- Try your hand at a non-stick pan if you have not already done so before. You will need far less fat for frying.
- Cook 'en papillote' (in paper parcels) to lock in moisture and flavour.
- Try cooking in a brick. This needs no fat. Chicken and fish are delicious this way.
- Grilling is light, tastes good and is better for your health than frying.
- Buy low-fat cheeses, which are better for the figure and the heart.
- Make using yogurt become second nature. Use on its own, with honey or fruit, or in cooking as a substitute for cream.
- Eat more vegetables and fruits (especially raw), grains, nuts and pulses.
- Make porridge part of your regular diet, with a couple of spoonfuls of extra oat bran.
- Choose sea salt. It tastes better and is better for you. Maldon salt does not need grinding.
- Save a fortune by giving convenience foods and commercially baked goods the go-by.
- Be sure to read labels when shopping for food to avoid unhealthy additives.
- Choose carefully in a restaurant; avoid fast food totally.

Follow these golden rules and you will already be on the road to a better diet and to lowering blood cholesterol.

FOODS WHICH POSITIVELY HELP

There are in fact a variety of foods which actually lower cholesterol; nature in her wisdom has, as it were, come up with the balancers. It's rather like the way dock leaves seemed to grow close to stinging nettles when we were children.

GRAINS, FRUITS, PULSES AND VEGETABLES are all high-fibre foods. Less protein and more of these foods in the diet will ensure adequate vitamins and mineral traces and a better way of eating. Increased vitality and resilience to illness are the benefits, along with a healthier heart. A high proportion of fibre in the diet will ensure good bowel function, eliminating harmful wastes and improving the metabolism. If possible, 75 to 80 per cent of these should be eaten raw (even in winter). Save time and fuel by undercooking vegetables to keep all their goodness. Choose food that is as unrefined as possible, buying raw and unrefined sugar and wholemeal bread instead of white. Refined flour should be avoided as it has lost almost all its goodness, vitamins and fibre, and is a nutritionless, constipating food.

APPLES have a wonderful, harmless cleansing effect – 'an apple a day . . .' Eaten raw and with the skin on, they should be part of the daily diet. If possible, make a habit of crunching the whole apple, eating everything except the stalk. It has a detoxifying effect that exceeds even a water fast. Few foods can be relied upon better to clear away the system of impurities and toxins and food sensitivities, and to help the appetite to return to normal when it has been confused by pollution (an evening in a smoke-filled room) or stress. An occasional day or two with nothing to eat but apples will give you a head start for a cholesterol-lowering programme.

NUTS AND SEEDS too are good for the condition of the heart. They are rich sources of vitamin E and fibre. Eating more of these, with pulses and vegetables, will result in less reliance on red meats for protein. They are high in minerals too, especially zinc. I keep a mix in the fridge which is a combination of sesame, pumpkin and sunflower seeds, combined briefly in a blender or food processor in equal quantities. It makes a crunchy topping for porridge, yogurt or stewed fruit, and I sometimes add another equal part of wheat germ for extra vitamin E.

GARLIC AND ONIONS are good for the heart. In India, Hindus disallow them on holy days, as they are thought to arouse the 'base passions'. In France onion soup is served to honeymoon couples on their wedding night. It is said to be 'fortifying'. (It is fascinating to notice how many traditionally aphrodisiac foods have a scientifically proven beneficial effect on the heart.)

Like onion, garlic is an antiseptic and is used to treat intestinal infections. It aids digestion and stimulates bile secretions, which then cause blood cholesterol to be called away to make more bile acids. This use of cholesterol takes it away from the blood, where it can build up and do mischief to the arteries.

For those who positively dislike the taste of garlic or who do not want their breath to smell of it, there are garlic capsules which are odourless. But it is said that if you eat enough of it, the digestion learns to cope perfectly and there is no whiff of garlic on the breath. In some Mediterranean countries there is a large amount of garlic in the cooking; for instance in the central and southern part of France, the Languedoc, where the tradition of cooking with garlic dates back to Roman times, a chicken dish with garlic (poulet béarnaise) is made by putting 2 lb (1 kg) of peeled cloves of garlic under the chicken before stewing it.

OLIVE OIL is nearly as old as the hills and has brought natural health and beauty to people of Mediterranean countries for many centuries. It is only quite recently that its goodness has been fully understood and that it is enjoyed almost worldwide.

The benefits of olive oil have always been obvious. The girl on the olive oil tin sums it up – epitomising good health with her shining black hair, golden skin and laughing mouth. An increasing interest in olive oil has led specialists in many fields of the medical profession to research the nutritional qualities of olive oil. This has brought to light the beneficial effects that it has on bone growth and brain development in both unborn and newborn babies. (Olive oil most closely resembles the fat in human milk.)

Olive oil, a monounsaturated fat, stands up best to rancidity, is stable under heat and is well tolerated in the human intestine.

Greek men are the most long-lived in Europe, and in spite of a fall in the consumption of olive oil, it is still the most widely used fat in Greece. A series of studies there shows that a very high level of olive oil consumption is accompanied both by very low cholesterol levels in the blood and low mortality rates due to CHD.

YOGURT is a wonder food, high in vitamins, protein and calcium and low in fat and calories. It is a versatile and invaluable food, being easily digested by young and old, marvellous on its own or as a basic ingredient in countless dishes. It is difficult to exaggerate the good qualities of yogurt.

As an ideal breakfast food, try yogurt with muesli and fruit; the rough with the smooth combination is a perfect start to the day. Fresh-flavoured, nourishing and easily digested, it is infinitely preferable to packaged breakfast cereals and fatty fried foods.

Yogurt is of immense value on a cholesterol-lowering diet as a substitute for cream or sour cream. Because yogurt is usually made from low-fat skimmed milk, and because the bacteria in yogurt converts the lactose (or sugar) in the milk to lactic acids, it contains fewer calories than whole milk and is an excellent food for slimmers. Natural yogurt contains more of the B vitamins thiamine and riboflavin than does milk, and also more protein.

Deliciously creamy and tart, it should be make full use of – with fruit, honey, nuts, raw vegetables and on its own. Combine it with fish, meat and poultry. Use it in vegetarian dishes to replace cream and soured cream. Be inventive and imaginative with yogurt and you will reap its benefits in flavour, looks and health.

It is worth shopping for the newest strain which is quite mildly soured with L. acidophilus and B. bifidum. These are believed to be so benign in the stomach and intestine as to actually help against food poisoning and listeria.

WATER is one important life-giving element that we hardly give a thought to. At least not until recently, now that the purity of our tap water is in doubt. We used to take it for granted and never dreamed that the day would come when we would have to buy our drinking water. It is the one sort of food that the body *cannot* do without. When Gandhi was on hunger strike, he still drank water, which kept him alive for an astonishing length of time.

Over half of our body weight is water. Water irrigates and flushes impurities away, regulates body temperature and has many other essential functions, such as aiding the digestion of food. We should make sure we drink plenty every day – usually thirst is the natural gauge of how much we need. Eat plenty of soups in winter, when we are less inclined to drink as much.

A religious sect known as the Essenes, who lived in the time of Jesus Christ, recognised the value of water-rich foods. They felt instinctively that light, water-filled fruits and vegetables and salads lifted the health of mind, body and soul. The water in these foods is not like tap or spring water, but it carries vital nutrients around the body.

Heavy, dense foods which do not carry much water tend to clog the system. Light salads, raw vegetables, sprouting seeds and fruits have the opposite effect. They are easily digested and do not stay in the stomach for long, transporting their nutrients around the body to be utilised for strength, energy and health.

THE SHOPPING BASKET

The selection of foods is where it all starts, and luckily there are many foods which are positively scrumptious as well as being good for us, so there is no need ever to feel deprived on a low-cholesterol diet.

To maintain a good diet requires a bit of thought and planning. The key is to draw on a variety of food types and in this way achieve balance. If the weekly menu includes poultry, fish and at least one vegetarian meal, and is not solely relying on red meat, this will automatically ensure that there is only a moderate amount of fat from meat. It is a good idea to get into the way of drawing on sources other than meat for daily protein. Nuts and beans are rich in protein and are best combined with a carbohydrate – rice and bean dishes, for example. However, nuts are high in fat (though not saturated fat) and should be limited. Fish is a low-cholesterol food which is protein rich. It also has potassium, zinc, iodine and trace elements.

In the dairy section it is a comparatively easy matter to stick to skimmed milk (break yourself in with semi-skimmed if you are used to full-cream milk). Even the simple change from whole to semi-skimmed milk can make a vast difference to the potential build-up of cholesterol. Semi-skimmed milk has less than half the butterfat of whole milk and thirty per cent fewer calories. Limit cheeses and choose only low-fat varieties. Use low-fat yogurt in place of cream.

Wholemeal breads are rich in B vitamins and fibre; it's best to buy no other kind. Most commercially baked goods such as cakes, buns and biscuits contain saturated fats, white flour and sugar, and you should give them the cold shoulder.

Maybe I should have *started* with the fruit and vegetables, because with these there is no need to exercise control, other than that dictated by the limits of your budget. (Buying less meat, fewer dairy products and baked goods will have cut spending already.) Here is a wealth of vitamins, minerals and fibre – and no cholesterol at all. 'Dirty' vegetables are best – they keep fresher with the protection of a little soil and they have not been washed in strange detergents.

Fruit and vegetables are often best bought in your local street market. There is better value there than in a supermarket where the packaging has to be paid for as well as all the other overheads. In the street market produce tends to be more seasonal and a greater percentage is home grown.

There are, of course, some other foods that do not come under any of these headings. An important one is oil – for cooking and for dressing salads. Olive oil is a wonderful food, high in monounsaturates but, like all fats, it is full of calories. Sunflower oil is pleasant for salad dressings and mayonnaise, and for a delicious luxury try nut oils. When it comes to salads, consider more low-fat yogurt dressings and the use of lemon juice and fresh herbs.

Get into the habit of reading labels when food shopping, watching out for fat content and for additives like preservatives and colouring. Skip luncheon meats; they tend to be very high in fats, although slices of cold roast turkey are fine and, surprisingly, so is ham (especially when the rim of fat is trimmed away). Bacon and sausages are too fatty and salty. Restrict the use of bacon to using it occasionally in a casserole for its flavour. Chicken breasts (skinned) are low in cholesterol, and veal is a leaner alternative to beef. Turkey breast is another low-fat meat, and so is game of all sorts. Beans (for alternative protein), rice, pasta and potatoes do not clock up calories and they supply carbohydrates. It was at one time thought, mistakenly, that these had to be restricted to control weight, but we know now that they actually help to metabolise fats correctly and are not in themselves fattening – only the foods we tend to eat with them.

Porridge oats and oat bran have actually been shown to

reduce cholesterol. Porridge has staged a big comeback, and oats are used in making muesli and oatcakes. A recent scientific survey of oatmeal in the US kept coming up with an unexpected (and unlooked for) finding, which was that porridge increases the libido. Try as they might, there was no escape from this one!

When buying muesli it is important to read the label and avoid ones with sugar, salt and other additives.

Enjoy shopping. Try not to be in too much of a hurry. Know what you are buying by reading labels.

A Shopping Checklist

Many foods not included in this list are equally good, but here are some that are easily available, economical and quick to prepare. Most importantly they *taste* good.

- wholemeal flour
- brown rice
- muesli (unless you make your own)
- nuts, like walnuts and hazelnuts
- tinned sardines and tuna fish
- wholemeal pasta
- dried fruits, like apricots
- oatmeal
- seeds, like sesame, pumpkin, sunflower
- tinned tomatoes, beans and chickpeas
- grains, like barley, bulghar
- olive oil, sunflower oil
- a few spices, coriander, caraway etc.
- mineral water
- honey

- dried peas and beans, lentils
- sea salt and peppercorns
- herbal teas, China tea
- Tamari or soy sauce
- vanilla pods, almond essence

Fresh foods
- wholemeal breads
- free-range eggs
- fresh fish
- fruit, vegetables
- lemons
- cottage and low-fat curd cheeses
- free-range chicken and game
- yogurt and skimmed milk
- salads and fresh herbs

I consider it a minor disaster to run out of lemons in the kitchen and have them on all shopping lists.

WEIGHTS CONVERSION SCALE

| | Metric | |
Imperial Ounces	Approx gram to nearest whole figure	Recommended conversion to nearest unit of 25
1	28	25
2	57	50
3	85	75
4	113	100
5	142	150
6	170	175
7	198	200
8	227	225
9	255	250
10	283	275
11	312	300
12	340	350
13	368	375
14	396	400
15	425	425
16	454	450
17	482	475
18	510	500
19	539	550
20	567	75

Pints	Approx ml to nearest whole figure	Recommended conversion to ml
¼	142	150
½	283	300
¾	425	450
1	567	600
1½	851	900
1¾	992	1000 (1 litre)

OVEN TEMPERATURE CHART

	°C	°F	Gas mark
Very cool	110	225	¼
	120	250	½
Cool	140	275	1
	150	300	2
Moderate	160	325	3
	180	350	4
Moderately hot	190	375	5
	200	400	6
Hot	220	425	7
	230	450	8
Very hot	240	475	9

Two
BREAKFASTS

The traditional English fried breakfast is notoriously bad for those who are watching their cholesterol intake and keeping a healthy heart. However, those who rely on a quick bowl of store-bought cereal or a slice of toast made with white bread are doing no better nutritionally. A healthy, satisfying breakfast provides a good start to the day and prevents mid-morning cravings for 'junk' snack food.

BREADS AND CEREALS are the most obvious choice for breakfast, so it is important to shop for the best and most nutritious. *Wholemeal* and *wholewheat* contain all the vitamins, minerals and fibre of the wheat grain. Brown bread is not necessarily wholemeal; it contains about 85 per cent of the wheat grain. Granary bread is not wholemeal, it is made of brown flour to which malted whole grains of wheat are added. So always buy wholemeal and wholewheat breads. Bread has the advantage that few nutrients are lost in baking apart from a small amount of vitamin B1. The only disadvantage of bread is the temptation to spread it with liberal amounts of butter or margarine. However, the nicer the bread the less one needs *on* it. Mediterranean countries hardly touch butter; perhaps it's because the bread tastes better.

WHOLEWHEAT CEREALS have usually lost a substantial amount of B vitamins in the cooking. They also have added sugar, and the higher up the list of ingredients sugar comes, the more there is. Shredded Wheat and Puffed Wheat and some mueslis have neither sugar nor salt added and are safest to stick to.

LOW-FAT MILK AND YOGURT are the best ways of ensuring enough calcium – and contain as much as do the higher-fat dairy products. Always buy 'live' yogurt. (It's 'live' unless the label says 'pasteurised'.)

FRESH FRUIT AND STEWED DRIED FRUIT are vital sources of fibre and full of vitamins, minerals and folic acids, weapons which defend us against disease.

OATS are a miracle food for many reasons but principally for their soluble fibre, which is different from the fibre of wheat bran. These two fibres act in different ways, the oat fibre gelling to ease the elimination of waste from the body. It also slows the rate at which the body converts food into blood sugar, giving a steadier flow of energy during the morning. This will affect mood, performance and appetite. This soluble fibre is most valuable too in cutting cholesterol. (I believe that the Scots, who now eat much less porridge oats than formerly, have a greatly increased incidence of heart disease.) Oats contain more oil than do other grains, and provide useful amounts of vitamin E and essential fatty acids.

MUESLI can be made from rolled oats, dried fruits and nuts. The advantage of making your own is that it will be all oats; commercial brands often have wheat flakes and, unless otherwise stated, added sugar and salt too.

PORRIDGE is best made from oatmeal (and not from 'instant' oats, which are pre-cooked and have lost some of their goodness in the process). Oatmeal has more flavour and more goodness. Rolled oats, although processed to an extent, are claimed to retain more of the food value. Soak coarse-cut oatmeal overnight in three times its volume of water in a glass or china bowl. Simmer for fifteen minutes in the morning in a non-aluminium saucepan.

OATCAKES are lovely for breakfast, or at any time with cheese, honey or marmalade.

HOME-MADE YOGURT

600 ml–1.15 litres/1–2 pints fresh skimmed milk
150 ml/¼ pint low-fat natural yogurt (1 small carton)

Bring the milk to full boil so that it rises to the top of the pan and remains there for 1–2 minutes. Cool to 43°C/110°F, or so that your finger can stay in it comfortably for at least 10 seconds. In a bowl stir the yogurt thoroughly into the warm milk and cover with clingfilm. Put into a warm place (or wide-mouthed Thermos, scalded and heated) for about 5–10 hours, depending on the warmth, or transfer to an electric yogurt maker. Take out as soon as it has set. Stir the yogurt again, re-cover and chill in the refrigerator. This chilling halts the activity of the bacteria. Keep back 3 tblsp for your next 'starter'.

Here are a few hints for a successful brew:

1   The 'starter' yogurt must be fresh, preferably not more than a day or two old, so buy from a supermarket with a fast turnover and examine the date mark. If you buy it from a small local shop, ask them the day of the week on which they take delivery of fresh yogurt, and buy and make your yogurt on that day.

2   Use clean utensils and equipment to inhibit activity from other bacteria.

3   The yogurt should be left undisturbed and away from vibrations while it is being made.

4   Natural yogurt will keep longer than yogurt to which fruit has been added. Natural yeasts in the fruit will cause the yogurt to become 'blown' or fizzy, so only add fruit the day the yogurt is to be eaten.

5   If your yogurt turns acid it is probably because it was incubated for too long, or at too high a temperature, or possibly a slightly stale carton of 'starter' yogurt was used in which the balance of bacteria had altered.

6   Thin 'sweet' yogurt is probably incubated at too low a temperature.

Dried lytholised milk ferments sold in sachets make a useful standby as they will keep for several years in a cool place, and can be used as a starter instead of fresh yogurt. But a carton of yogurt is much less costly and produces equally good results.

Your yogurt will not be quite so uniformly smooth as commercial yogurt, because it has not been homogenised. It may also be thinner because commercial yogurt has 12–16 per cent added milk solids. You can thicken yours with the addition of 1 tblsp of skimmed milk powder to 600ml/1 pint milk. Add this at the start of yogurt-making. Longlife UHT skimmed milk is very useful for making yogurt as it is already sterile, so simply warm to blood heat and add the starter yogurt. Treat as fresh milk from this point on.

All the recipes in this book are made using the basic natural yogurt, without sweetening or flavouring, but once you have made your basic yogurt you can vary the flavour and texture in all sorts of ways; mix it with freshly chopped fruit, or a sweetened purée of cooked fruit, fresh or dried, add chopped nuts, raisins and sultanas, stir in honey or jam, or simply soft brown sugar, to sweeten. For a savoury dish it is delicious mixed with just a few freshly chopped herbs from the garden, finely chopped olives or onions, or even a little curry powder.

Making your own yogurt means that you always have plenty for yourself and your family. It is less expensive, and I am convinced that the flavour is better.

SOFT CURD CHEESE

(makes 225g/8oz)

2.25 litres/4 pints skimmed milk
300ml/½ pint natural low-fat yogurt
1 tblsp rennet

Sterilise all equipment before beginning.

Heat the milk to blood heat and add the yogurt and rennet. Pour into a clear bowl, cover and leave in a warm place to set (8–10 hours). Strain off the whey, put the curd into a muslin or fine cotton bag and strain again (a colander or sieve is ideal for this purpose). Leave for 1 hour and then replace with fresh muslin. Allow to drip again until the dripping stops (approximately 2 hours). Replace with fresh muslin and chill in the refrigerator before using.

This can be eaten just as it is. It can also be used to thicken a sauce that might otherwise call for egg yolks or cream; substituted for cream cheese in recipes; eaten with bread, biscuits or oatcakes; mixed with fresh herbs; or shaped into a ball and rolled in finely chopped parsley or coarsely ground black pepper.

HOME-MADE MUESLI
(makes about 1.25 kg/2½ lb)

Here is a basic muesli recipe, which I mix with fruit and yogurt. Store it in an airtight container. Multiply by four if you eat it regularly and are a big family.

450 g/1 lb medium oatmeal
2 tblsp chopped walnuts
2 tblsp chopped hazelnuts
100 g/4 oz dried vine fruits (raisins etc.)
100 g/4 oz ground almonds

Mix all ingredients together. Add anything else to your own taste, e.g. chopped dates. This is good with milk or apple juice, or serve it with a bowl of yogurt and some fresh or stewed dried fruit. A teaspoon of wheatgerm on each serving ensures some extra B1 and E vitamins for the day. (Keep the wheatgerm packet in the fridge.)

Soaking the muesli in apple juice overnight helps to release the enzymes.

APPLE MUESLI
For each serving

1 dessertspoon runny honey
2 tblsp apple juice or orange juice
1 dessert apple, grated
2 tblsp low-fat yogurt
2 tblsp muesli
Squeeze of lemon juice

Mix the honey and the juices together and pour them over the grated apple. Combine this with the yogurt and muesli. It can be prepared the night before, or make it at breakfast time if you prefer it to be crunchy.

PEP-UP BREAKFAST

I have this for breakfast nearly every day. The yogurt provides protein and seems to last me OK until lunchtime.

For each serving

150 ml/¼ pint low-fat yogurt
a piece of fruit (a pear, clementine, kiwi fruit, apple etc.)
*1 tblsp mixed ground seeds
1 tblsp wheatgerm
1 tsp honey

Put the yogurt into a bowl. Peel (if necessary) and chop the fruit and put it into the yogurt. Add the ground seeds, wheatgerm and honey.

Enjoy! It is strangely fresh, appetising and satisfying.

*The ground seeds are pumpkin, sesame and sunflower briefly whizzed in a blender and kept in the fridge in a screwtop jar with the wheatgerm. If you like, they can be mixed together in equal proportions – say, 4 tablespoons of each.

CITRUS SALAD

(serves 4)

This can provide much-needed vitamin C in the depths of winter!

2 pink grapefruit
2 oranges
2 clementines
1 tsp runny honey

Wash and peel the fruit. Cut out the grapefruit sections, removing the flesh from the membrane. Do the same to the oranges. Cut the clementines across. Mix all together gently with the honey.

HOT GRAPEFRUIT

The only grapefruit that I really like are those pink ones from Texas that cost an arm and a leg but don't need sugar. Nevertheless, these suggestions will do for the ordinary face-wrinkling sort of grapefruit just as well as the pink kind.

Halve the grapefruit and loosen each section with a grapefruit knife. Pick out any pips with a teaspoon.

Now . . .

Sprinkle with soft brown sugar
Or . . . chopped roasted hazelnuts or walnuts with sugar
Or . . . brown sugar with ground cinnamon
Or . . . sweet sherry, Madeira or Marsala (for breakfast? Sure, why not?)
Or . . . chopped stem ginger with a teaspoon or two of its own syrup
Put your grapefruit with its topping under a fairly hot grill for a few minutes until the surface is bubbling. Give it long enough for the grapefruit to heat right through.

ANGELA'S APRICOTS

(serves 4 or more)

1 packet (225 g/8 oz) dried apricots
1 Earl Grey tea-bag
boiling water

The night before tuck an Earl Grey tea-bag (or any scented, fragrant tea – Lapsang Souchong would be lovely too) into the apricots in a bowl.

Pour on boiling water to cover.

Leave to soak until the following morning, by which time they will be ready to eat with yogurt. A bowl of chopped nuts and some honey can be added for variety.

GRILLED TOMATOES ON TOAST

This is almost too simple to mention, but it is just so delicious and one forgets about things and comes back to them again – so no more apologies for this old favourite.

Halve ripe tomatoes, sprinkle them with black pepper and a few drops of oil, and grill. Spread fresh, hot wholemeal toast with a little Marmite (optional) and lay the tomatoes on top. Strewn with a few basil leaves or mint, parsley or thyme, this is transformed into a light luncheon or supper dish. They can also be grilled with grated low-fat cheese on top.

For those who like or feel they need more protein in the morning, substitute baked beans in the above recipe. Shop for a brand without sugar.

GRILLED SARDINES

This may be difficult to face first thing, and is perhaps better suited to a leisurely brunch at the weekend.

Rinse and dry fresh sardines. Sprinkle them with lemon juice and spread with Dijon mustard. Roll them in wholemeal breadcrumbs and grill, with a sprinkling of oil, until done. Season with salt and pepper and serve with a lemon wedge and some grilled tomatoes.

CHEESE MUFFINS

(serves 2)

2 bran or wholemeal muffins
1 banana
4 tblsp low-fat curd cheese
½ tsp cinnamon
1 tsp runny honey

Split the muffins and toast them lightly. Mix together the sliced banana, cinnamon and cottage cheese. Pile this mixture on to the split muffins and drizzle a little honey on the top.

Put under the grill for a few minutes and eat hot.

WANDA'S OATCAKES

600 ml/1 pint medium oatmeal, slightly 'liquidised'
in a blender or food processor
300 ml/½ pint self-raising flour
200 g/7 oz low-cholesterol margarine
2 tsp soft brown sugar
¼ tsp sea salt
1 tblsp wheatgerm
1 tblsp pinhead porridge oats

Mix all ingredients and knead lightly, adding a little warm water to make a soft dough. Roll out (not too thinly) on a board dusted with wholemeal flour. Cut into rounds the size of large scones and place on an ungreased tin. Prick with a fork to allow the heat to penetrate to the centre easily.

Cook in oven (180°C, Gas Mark 4, 350°F) for about half an hour.

FLUMMERY

'To make a pretty sort of Flummery: put three handfuls of fine oatmeal into two quarts of water, let it steep a day and night, then pour off the clear water through a fine sieve, and boil it down till it is as thick as hasty pudding. Put in sugar to taste and a spoonful of orangeflower water. Pour it into a shallow dish to set for your use.'

Serve this as a light, less wintry alternative to porridge. It is good with yogurt or with a small jugful of sweetened blackberry juice.

SMOKED HADDOCK AND TOMATO PANCAKES

(serves 2–3)

Basic pancake batter (see p. 75)

Make the pancakes and keep them warm while you prepare the filling.

Filling
1 tblsp grated Parmesan cheese
3 tomatoes, skinned, deseeded and chopped
300 ml/½ pint white sauce (see p. 195)
225 g/8 oz smoked haddock (or cod), cooked and flaked
freshly ground black pepper

Stir the Parmesan and tomatoes into the white sauce. Reserve 4 tablespoons of this sauce mixture and add the cooked, flaked haddock to the rest. Spread the sauce on to the pancakes and roll the pancakes up. Place them side by side in a greased, heatproof dish and spoon the reserved sauce over them. Place into a moderate oven to heat through until the pancakes are golden brown.

HERRINGS IN OATMEAL

This is a Scottish way of preparing herrings and very good it is too. The backbone of the herring can quite easily be removed by laying out the cleaned fish, skin side uppermost, and giving it a good bash down the backbone with your hand or a rolling pin. Turn the fish over and gently pull away the backbone and most of the bones. Remove the remaining ones that you can get at, with a pair of pincers.

Brush the herring with lemon juice and roll it in medium oatmeal. It is best to use ordinary oatmeal, not rolled oats.

Place under the grill and cook on both sides until done.

Season and serve with lemon wedges.

KEDGEREE

(serves 4)

Traditionally served at breakfast, kedgeree is also delicious for lunch or supper.

0.5 kg/1 lb smoked cod, soaked in cold water
1 small onion, finely chopped
2 tblsp olive oil
½ tsp curry powder
175 g/6 oz long-grain rice
1 bay leaf
freshly ground black pepper
juice of 1 lemon
3 tblsp chopped parsley
lemon wedges to serve

Skin the cod, then bring it barely to the boil in fresh water, and simmer for a few minutes until tender. Drain and flake. Cook the onion in the oil until soft and golden. Add the curry powder and cook for a minute longer.

Meanwhile, cook the rice in plenty of boiling salted water, with the bay leaf, for 10 minutes. Drain and sprinkle with a few drops of cold water to separate the grains and stop the rice cooking. Combine the flaked cod, the onion mixture and the rice. Grind plenty of black pepper into the kedgeree and sprinkle with the lemon juice and parsley. Toss lightly and pile into a hot dish.

Serve with lemon wedges.

Optional: A few spoonfuls of yogurt can be added at the end.

Three
SOUPS

Fresh soups are healthy and offer such a variety of choice that they are right for almost any occasion. They can be served chilled or hot, chunky or clear, thick or thin, elegant or hearty. Eaten with fresh bread they make an easy, delicious lunch; add a salad and you have a nourishing supper. By themselves, the lighter ones are an ideal choice as a starter for more elaborate dinners, and some of the soups included at the end of this section are one-pot dishes – meals in themselves!

Fresh vegetables, herbs and stock (either meat or vegetable) make the basis of countless different soups. Some vegetables, like Jerusalem artichokes, can be cooked in milk and the flavour is even better. Keep the cooking liquor from vegetables. Boil the carcass of a cooked chicken with onion, some parsley stalks and a carrot to make a lovely broth. Strain and cool. Skim the fat off the top. This chicken stock can be stored in the freezer until needed.

Yogurt is an invaluable piquant addition to many soups and using it as a substitute for cream or soured cream makes soup an additionally healthy choice for the heart-conscious eater.

To prevent yogurt from curdling and separating in a hot soup, mix 1–2 teaspoons of cornflour with a little yogurt in a cup and add this first to the hot soup. Then stir in the rest of the yogurt and reheat but do not boil.

Allow the flavours to blend and intensify by leaving the basic soup to stand for two hours or more before reheating and adding the garnish.

Plan your soups around the fresh vegetables and ingredients of the season, when they are at their most tempting. Garnish them with a bright contrasting colour such as fresh, chopped parsley or chives, or a swirl of yogurt.

GAZPACHO
(serves 4)

Gazpacho is a Spanish cold soup which dates back hundreds of years. It was probably brought to Spain by the Romans, and did not include tomatoes until the discovery of the New World. The name may come from the Latin *caspa*, which means a small piece, and refers to the broken bits of bread which have always been a main ingredient. It is typical Andalusian fare.

The flavour of gazpacho in Spain depends on the red, sun-ripened tomatoes and green peppers and cucumbers that are so sweet-smelling and warm straight from the plant. It tastes good here, but not quite the same. Try to find ripe vegetables grown in a garden not a greenhouse.

3 slices white bread, crusts removed
6 large tomatoes, peeled and deseeded
1–2 sweet peppers, deseeded and chopped
1 medium onion, finely diced
1 medium cucumber, finely diced
1 clove garlic, crushed
3 tblsp olive oil
1 tblsp wine vinegar
sea salt and freshly ground black pepper
600 ml/1 pint water

Remove crusts from bread and break into small pieces. Put into a bowl with the tomatoes, sweet peppers, onion, cucumber, garlic, oil and vinegar. Add salt and pepper. Pour on the water. Leave to stand for 1 hour.

Put into a blender and whizz very briefly (don't allow the soup to become too fine in texture). Put into the fridge with 2 lumps of ice added.

Small bowls of chopped tomatoes, onions, sweet peppers and small croutons of fried bread for garnish are often served with the soup.

TARATOR

(serves 4)

This yogurt and cucumber soup is from Bulgaria, and
a very similar one, cacik, is Turkish.

1 medium cucumber, peeled
1 tsp sea salt
1 clove garlic, crushed
600 ml/1 pint low-fat yogurt
50 g/2 oz walnuts, very thinly chopped
freshly ground white pepper
2 tblsp fresh mint leaves, finely chopped
(*or* 2 tblsp fresh dill, finely chopped)
1 tsp sugar
1 tsp white wine vinegar

Peel the cucumber and cut into half lengthwise. Scoop out the
seeds with a teaspoon. Grate the cucumber flesh coarsely and
sprinkle with salt. Place in a colander and leave to drain over a
plate for about 30 minutes.

A few hours before serving mix the cucumber, crushed garlic,
yogurt and walnuts together. Add some freshly ground pepper
(white peppercorns if you have them).

Put the mint into a cup and bruise it with the sugar, using
the back of a spoon. Add the vinegar and tip into the soup.
Leave it to mature for a while before serving.

DIPLOMAT SOUP

(serves 6)

A chilled soup; this is a tomato and yogurt cooler
from Washington D.C.

2 tblsp sunflower oil
2 onions, peeled and chopped
1 medium cucumber, peeled, deseeded and cubed
1.2 litres/2 pints tomato juice
freshly chopped basil to taste
300 ml/½ pint chicken stock
sea salt and freshly ground pepper
300 ml/½ pint low-fat yogurt
sprigs of mint to garnish

Heat the oil and gently cook the onions until soft but not brown.
Add the cucumber, tomatoes and basil. Cover and simmer for
10 minutes, then pour in the stock and simmer for a further 10
minutes. Liquidise in the blender and push through a sieve,
discarding any pips. Cool. Season to taste and stir in yogurt.
Chill the soup and garnish with mint sprigs to serve.

ICED CUCUMBER SOUP

(serves 6)

1 small onion, finely chopped
2 tblsp sunflower oil
1 large cucumber, peeled and sliced
3 medium potatoes, sliced
900 ml/1½ pints light chicken stock
salt and white pepper
2 tblsp fromage frais
chopped mint to garnish

Soften the onion in the oil, then add the cucumber and potato.
Cook very gently for 10 minutes, stirring from time to time,
without browning. Add the stock and bring to the boil. Cover
and simmer gently for 20 minutes (not more).

Press through a sieve or blend in the liquidiser and pour into
a bowl to cool. Adjust seasoning when the soup is cold. Just
before serving, stir in the fromage frais and garnish with chopped mint. Serve chilled with hot crusty rolls.

COURGETTE AND CUCUMBER SOUP

(serves 6)

1 cucumber, roughly chopped
equal weight of courgettes, chopped
900 ml/1½ pints chicken stock
150 ml/¼ pint low-fat yogurt
snipped chives to garnish

Simmer the cucumber and courgettes in the stock for 15 minutes.
Blend with the yogurt in the liquidiser or press through a sieve.
Reheat or serve chilled with a pinch of chives.

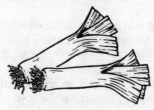

VICHYSSOISE

(serves 6)

This is an elegant chilled soup, an ideal starter for a summer
dinner party. Served hot, with skimmed milk in place of the
yogurt, it becomes potage bonne femme, a comforting and
delicious winter soup.

4 large leeks
1 small onion, chopped
2 tblsp sunflower oil
3 medium potatoes, sliced
900 ml/1½ pints chicken stock
sea salt and white pepper
150 ml/¼ pint low-fat yogurt
snipped chives to garnish

Wash, trim and chop the leeks. Soften with the onion in the oil,
without browning. Add the potatoes and cook gently for a
further 5 minutes. Pour in the stock and season to taste. Bring
to the boil, cover and simmer for 20 minutes. Press through a
sieve or blend in the liquidiser. Cool and stir in the yogurt.
    Serve chilled, sprinkled with chives.

FRIENDLY HALL SWEET PEPPER SOUP

(serves 4–5)

This used to be served cold in my father's house in Barbados, but it is also good hot.

1 onion, peeled and finely chopped
225 g/8 oz green peppers, deseeded and finely chopped
2 tblsp sunflower oil
1 (298 g/10½ oz) can consommé
1 tsp cornflour
600 ml/1 pint low-fat yogurt
chopped peppers to garnish

Soften the onion and peppers in the oil for a few minutes without browning. Add the consommé, bring to the boil, then cover and simmer for 10 minutes. Slake the cornflour in a little yogurt and stir into the soup. Continue simmering for 2 minutes to cook the cornflour. Cool and mix in the rest of the yogurt. Garnish with a few chopped peppers on the top.

CHILLED PEA AND MINT SOUP

(serves 6)

1 small onion, peeled and thinly sliced
1 bay leaf
½ chicken stock cube
900 ml/1½ pints skimmed milk
225 g/8 oz fresh or frozen peas
grated rind of ½ lemon
1 tblsp chopped mint
4 mint sprigs to garnish

Simmer the onion with the bay leaf in milk for 10 minutes. Remove the bay leaf and add the peas, stock cube and fresh mint. Simmer for about 10 minutes, or until the peas are cooked. Liquidise or sieve and, when the soup has cooled, set aside in the fridge to chill.

Garnish with a swirl of yogurt and a sprig of mint.

CHILLED AVOCADO SOUP

(serves 4)

2 ripe avocados
1–2 tblsp lemon juice
600 ml/1 pint chicken stock, skimmed of all fat
150 ml/¼ pint low-fat yogurt
sea salt and pepper
5–6 drops Tabasco
chopped chives

Halve the avocados and take out the stones. With a teaspoon, scoop the flesh into a blender. Add the lemon juice, chicken stock, yogurt, seasoning and Tabasco.

Liquidise, pour into a bowl and put in the fridge to chill. It cannot, however, be made more than a couple of hours ahead of serving as it loses its lovely delicate green colour.

Serve with a good pinch of chopped chives in each bowl.

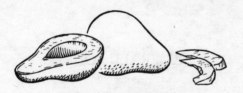

SLIMMER'S SOUP

(serves 2)

I often have this at lunchtime as a quick meal in a glass.

300 ml/½ pint yogurt
300 ml/½ pint tomato juice
1 egg
juice of ½ lemon
a little sea salt and some black pepper
a few sprigs of watercress (optional)

Combine all the ingredients except the watercress with a whisk or a blender. Pour into glasses or bowls and put sprigs of watercress in the centre of each.

POTAGE CRÈME SEYCHELLES

(serves 4–6)

1.2 litres/2 pints good chicken stock
1 small pineapple
2 tblsp sunflower oil
1 tblsp flour
2 tsp ground cumin seeds
150 ml/¼ pint low-fat yogurt
sea salt and pepper
1 tblsp freshly chopped coriander leaves
1 tblsp freshly chopped chives

Heat the chicken stock. Peel and core the pineapple and crush the flesh into a blender or food processor, or chop it finely.

Heat the oil in a saucepan and stir in the flour and cumin to make a roux. Add the stock, stirring and simmering. Mix in the pineapple flesh and set aside to cool. When cold stir in the yogurt, seasoning to taste and coriander and chives. Serve chilled.

EMERALD SOUP

(serves 8)

1 large Spanish onion
50 g/2 oz butter
1 head lettuce
1 bunch watercress
100 g/4 oz spinach (barely cooked)
1 tblsp chopped parsley
grated rind of 1 lemon
2 tblsp flour
2 litres/3½ pints chicken stock
150 ml/¼ pint low-fat yogurt
salt and pepper

Soften the onion in butter and then throw in the washed and torn head of lettuce. Pick over the watercress and discard the large stems; wash it in cold water. Add these leaves to the onion and lettuce and stir in the spinach, parsley and lemon rind. After a couple of minutes sprinkle the flour on to this and mix it in well. Add the chicken stock (skimmed and strained) and bring the soup to the boil.

Swirl in the yogurt and allow all the soup to boil for one minute only. Take off the heat and liquidise and sieve. Taste carefully and season sparingly. Serve hot, lukewarm or cold. Don't allow the soup to boil for more than a few seconds when you reheat it.

This is a really beautiful soup but is best eaten within a day of making it.

GREEK SOUP

This is very good if you are cold or tired as it could hardly be quicker to make.

For each person: Take ½ pint of skimmed chicken stock and bring it to the boil. (Alternatively, mix half a chicken stock cube – or a heaped teaspoon of Vegetal [obtainable from health food stores] – with a mug of boiling water.) Break an egg into the bottom of a warm bowl and whisk it with a fork. Now pour the hot soup gently on to this, whisking as you go. Finally add a *good* squeeze of lemon juice – about a quarter of a lemon.

WINTER VEGETABLE SOUP

(serves 6)

50 g/2 oz sunflower oil
1 large onion, peeled and finely chopped
225 g/8 oz carrots, chopped
225 g/8 oz parsnips, chopped
175 g/6 oz turnips, chopped
175 g/6 oz swede, chopped
2 sticks celery, finely chopped
6 tomatoes, peeled and chopped
1 generous litre/2 pints chicken or beef stock
a small bay leaf
2 tblsp chopped parsley
salt and freshly ground black pepper

Melt the oil in a heavy-bottomed saucepan and add all the chopped vegetables. Cook gently, stirring for 10 minutes. Add the stock and bay leaf to the vegetables and bring to the boil. Cover and simmer for 15–20 minutes. Sprinkle with the parsley and season to taste.

TOMATO SOUP WITH
GARLIC AND TARRAGON

(serves 4)

A swift one.

1 onion, finely chopped
1 clove garlic, crushed
2–3 tblsp olive oil
1 pack (450 g/16 oz) passata (chopped, sieved tomatoes)
salt and pepper
1 tblsp chopped tarragon

Soften the onion and garlic in olive oil, then cook for another 10–15 minutes with the passata. Whizz in a blender. Season to taste. Reheat to serve. The soup can be thinned with a little water if necessary. Sprinkle with the fresh tarragon.

MUSHROOM SOUP

(serves 6)

50 g/2 oz butter
1 medium onion, peeled and thinly sliced
1 clove garlic, crushed
450 g/1 lb button mushrooms, thinly sliced
juice of ½ lemon
2 tblsp flour
1.2 litres/2 pints chicken stock
1 chicken bouillon cube
freshly ground black pepper
a little low-fat yogurt
1 tsp paprika

Put the butter in a good thick-bottomed saucepan with the onion and crushed clove of garlic and cook gently over a low heat so that the garlic does not burn. The onion should be soft and transparent. Meanwhile sprinkle the lemon juice on the mushroom slices.

Now add the mushrooms to the saucepan and turn everything about together over the heat for about 5 minutes. Sprinkle the flour on to this and stir carefully for a few minutes.

Pour in some chicken stock and the crumbled cube. Bring to the boil and stir well. Add the rest of the stock and simmer gently for 15 minutes. Purée in a blender.

Add pepper and taste for seasoning.

Reheat to serve and put a spoonful of yogurt in each helping, with a pinch of paprika on the top.

WALNUT SOUP

(serves 6)

175 g/6 oz shelled walnuts
1 clove garlic, crushed
900 ml/1½ pints hot chicken stock
sea salt and white pepper
150 ml/¼ pint low-fat yogurt
chopped parsley to garnish

Put the walnuts and garlic into the liquidiser with a little stock, and blend to a creamy consistency. Turn into a saucepan, gradually stir in the remaining stock and heat through. Season to taste.

Remove from the heat and stir in the yogurt. Serve garnished with chopped parsley.

CELERY AND ALMOND SOUP

(serves 6)

1 good head celery, washed and chopped
2 onions, finely chopped
a little chopped thyme
1 litre/1¾ pints chicken stock
black pepper, sea salt and a little grated nutmeg
100 g/4 oz ground almonds
a spoonful or two of low-fat yogurt
chopped fresh coriander leaves to garnish

Simmer the celery, onions and thyme in well-skimmed stock for about 35–40 minutes and season lightly. Liquidise the soup with the almonds and taste to check the seasoning. Swirl a spoonful or two of yogurt into the soup and sprinkle with chopped coriander.

This is lovely served hot or cold.

PARSLEY SOUP

(serves 6–8)

2 large Spanish onions
1 kg/2 lb potatoes
1 small bay leaf
2 litres/3½ pints chicken stock
grated zest of 1 lemon
sea salt and freshly ground pepper
1 good large bunch parsley, finely chopped

Peel and slice the onions and potatoes and put into a pan with the bay leaf and stock. Simmer for half an hour. Liquidise or sieve. Add the lemon zest, seasoning and parsley and simmer for 5 to 10 minutes. Serve hot.

LEEK AND POTATO SOUP

(serves 4–6)

This is known in France as 'potage bonne femme'
or 'good woman soup'.

50 g/2 oz butter
1 small onion
4 medium leeks, chopped and well washed
1 stick celery (optional), chopped very small
1 carrot, washed and grated
2 medium potatoes, peeled and thinly sliced
1 litre/1¾ pints chicken stock (or water and 1 cube)
seasoning (go easy)
chopped parsley for sprinkling
a little yogurt

Melt the butter in a good saucepan and soften the onion in it gently. Add the leeks, celery, grated carrot and potatoes. Sauté them in the butter, stirring occasionally to prevent sticking. Now add the stock. Bring to the boil and simmer gently for 20 minutes. Liquidise just half the soup in a blender, then return it to the rest – or use a potato masher in the saucepan to purée some of the vegetables and make the soup a little thick and creamy.

Just before serving, swirl in a little yogurt. Sprinkle with parsley.

LENTIL SOUP

(serves 6)

Lentil soup is both inexpensive and nourishing. Pulses are rich in protein so it is a good soup to put in a Thermos for a packed lunch. Fry cubes of bread in a little sunflower oil with a clove of garlic and drain the fried bread cubes on a piece of kitchen paper. The old-fashioned name for these is 'sippets'. Pack the sippets separately so that they are crisp when put into the soup.

1 medium onion, peeled and finely chopped
1 leek, trimmed, chopped and washed
2 cloves garlic, crushed
2 medium potatoes, peeled and thinly sliced
150 g/6 oz lentils
2 litres/3½ pints water
1 bacon or ham bone
10 peppercorns

Rinse the lentils well under cold water and pick out anything that doesn't look right (you sometimes find little bits of stone and grit).

Put all the ingredients into a pan and simmer for 50–60 minutes, covered. Fish out the bacon bone and peppercorns and discard them. Add a little water to the soup if it seems too thick.

I often cook this in a pressure cooker instead of the conventional way. It takes 20 minutes.

Serve with the garlic-flavoured sippets.

FRENCH ONION SOUP

(serves 6)

4 large Spanish onions, finely chopped
3 tblsp sunflower oil
1 generous litre/2 pints beef stock
1 tsp sugar
sea salt and freshly ground black pepper
6 slices French bread
100 g/4 oz Edam cheese, grated
1 tblsp brandy
chopped parsley to garnish

Cook the onions in the oil in a thick-bottomed covered pan for at least 20 minutes, turning frequently. They should be quite soft. Simmer with the stock, sugar, salt and pepper for a further 30 minutes.

Meanwhile, toast the bread slices in the oven, then heap the grated cheese on top and brown under the grill. Now stir the brandy into the soup. Serve the soup into the bowls and place a cheesy bread slice in each. Sprinkle with chopped parsley.

SIMPLE JERUSALEM ARTICHOKE SOUP

(serves 6)

Some vegetable soups seem even better when made with milk rather than stock. It keeps the fine, delicate flavour.

0.75 kg/1½ lb Jerusalem artichokes
1 tblsp sunflower oil
1 generous litre/2 pints skimmed milk
sea salt and white pepper
chopped parsley to garnish

Carefully scrape and chop the artichokes. Cook gently in the oil and margarine in a heavy-bottomed saucepan, stirring frequently, until soft. Add a little milk if they start to turn brown. When soft, blend the artichokes in the liquidiser with some of the milk, or press through a sieve. Return the purée to the saucepan, stir in the remaining milk and bring to the boil. Cover and simmer for 10 minutes. Taste and adjust for seasoning and sprinkle with chopped parsley.

JERUSALEM ARTICHOKE
AND TOMATO SOUP

(serves 4)

This soup has a pretty, soft pink colour and a lovely flavour.

1 small onion, finely chopped
1 tblsp sunflower oil
450 g/1 lb artichokes, sliced
600 ml/1 pint tomato juice
½ chicken cube
chopped coriander leaves

Cook the onion in oil for a few minutes and add the artichokes. (There is no need to peel the artichokes if they are young enough; they need only be well scrubbed.)

Pour in the tomato juice, add the chicken cube and simmer for about 20 minutes. Liquidise in the blender. Taste for seasoning.

Serve sprinkled with chopped coriander.

Small croutons of fried bread are good with this one too.

SISTER-IN-LAW SOUP

(serves 4)

Louise is a wonderful gardener (the house is never without fresh vegetables) and an excellent cook – my brother is a happy man!

1 small onion, finely chopped
225 g/½ lb potatoes (peeled weight)
225 g/½ lb parsnips (peeled weight)
600 ml/1 pint skimmed milk
1 chicken cube (optional)
chopped parsley or snipped chives

Simmer everything except the fresh herbs together for about 25 minutes or until the vegetables are soft. Liquidise or sieve.

Serve sprinkled with chopped herbs.

This soup has a lovely, mild flavour and really tastes of the vegetables.

SOUPE AU PISTOU
(SOUP WITH BASIL)

(serves 6)

1 large onion, finely chopped
1 small tin of haricot beans, drained
225 g/8 oz French beans, sliced
175 g/6 oz courgettes, washed and sliced
3 medium carrots, grated
1 large potato, peeled and cut into small cubes
100 g/4 oz peas
2 large (beef) tomatoes, peeled, deseeded and chopped
water, sea salt and pepper

Pistou sauce
2 large cloves garlic, crushed
a generous handful of basil, stripped off its stems
olive oil (about 4 tblsp)
grated Parmesan cheese (about 2 tblsp)
crushed black pepper

Put all the soup ingredients into a saucepan and add enough fresh water to cover the vegetables by a couple of inches. Bring to the boil and simmer, skimming occasionally, until the vegetables are well done. (If you can, slip the peas and tomatoes in just 5 minutes before the end of the cooking time.) Season and taste.

Blend all the pistou ingredients in a liquidiser or work them together in the order given.

Put a soupspoonful of pistou in the bottom of warm soup bowls and ladle the soup over. Serve crusty bread with this, and offer more pistou separately.

BORSCH

(serves 6)

Borsch can either be clear or contain vegetables; the version I give here is a hearty soup with all the vegetables in it.

2 raw beetroots, peeled and grated
2 onions, peeled and chopped
2 large carrots, scraped and grated
1 parsnip, peeled and grated
2 leeks, white parts only, washed and chopped
1 clove garlic, crushed
1 bouquet garni (celery stalk, sprig of thyme and bay leaf, tied together)
2.25 litres/4 pints mutton or ham stock, skimmed of all fat
150 g/5 oz cabbage, shredded
3 tomatoes, peeled and chopped
1 tsp sugar, sea salt and freshly ground black pepper
2 tblsp chopped parsley
300 ml/½ pint low-fat yogurt
1 tblsp flour
150 ml/¼ pint soured cream (optional)

Put the first seven ingredients into a large pan with the stock. Bring to the boil, cover and simmer for 20 minutes. Now add the cabbage, tomatoes, sugar, seasoning and parsley and cook gently for a further 30 minutes. Work the yogurt and flour together until they are quite smooth. Stir into the soup and heat over a low heat for 5 minutes.

Just before serving, swirl in the soured cream.

QUICK SPINACH SOUP

(serves 4)

Groucho Marx said that 'the world would be a better place for children if the grown-ups ate the spinach'.

1 small onion
2 tblsp sunflower oil
1 tblsp flour
225 g/8 oz finely chopped frozen spinach, defrosted
600 ml/1 pint chicken or veal stock
150 ml/¼ pint low-fat yogurt
grated nutmeg (optional)

Soften the onion in the oil. Stir in the flour and cook for 1 minute. Stir in the spinach and cook over low heat for 3 minutes, stirring. Add the stock, bring to the boil, cover and simmer gently for 10 minutes.

Just before serving, remove from the heat and stir in the yogurt.

Add a light dusting of grated nutmeg if you are fond of it.

SMOKED HADDOCK SOUP

(serves 6)

50 g/2 oz butter
225 g/8 oz onions, chopped
150 ml/¼ pint sherry
1 carrot, grated
1 stick of celery, finely chopped
freshly ground pepper
1 generous litre/2 pints skimmed milk
1 kg/2 lb smoked haddock
(soaked in water, skinned and chopped)
low-fat yogurt to garnish

Soften the onions in the butter. Add the sherry, grated vegetables and pepper. Simmer, covered, for 5 to 10 minutes. Add the milk and smoked haddock.

Simmer for half an hour. Liquidise and sieve.

Garnish with a good dollop of yogurt.

FISH SOUP

(serves 6)

2 kg/4 lb fish bones and fish heads
2 litres/3½ pints fresh water
3 tblsp olive oil
1 large leek (its white and pale green part), chopped
1 large carrot, grated
2 sticks celery, finely chopped
450 g/1 lb potatoes (weighed when peeled), thinly sliced
100 g/¼ lb button mushrooms, chopped
1 fresh red chilli pepper (its hot seeds removed)
sea salt and fresh black pepper
2 good sprigs of thyme or lemon thyme
3 tblsp plain flour
2 tsp tomato purée
450 g/1 lb fresh fillets (skinned weight) of
mullet, whiting or cod
4 tomatoes (skin and pips removed), chopped
grated rind of 1 lemon
rounds of French bread
150 ml/¼ pint mayonnaise (see p. 192)
1 clove garlic
¼ tsp dried chilli flakes
plenty of chopped parsley

Simmer the fish bones and heads in the water for 40 minutes.
Strain. Discard all the fish pieces. Melt the oil in a good-sized
pan and cook the leek, carrot, celery, potatoes, mushrooms and
chopped chilli peppers in this for 10 minutes, turning occasionally with a wooden spoon so that it does not stick or brown.
Season and add the fresh thyme, pulled off its stalks. Shake the
flour over this and mix together well. Add the tomato purée.

Now pour the fish stock on to the vegetables and stir and
bring to the boil. Simmer for 20 minutes. Chop the fish fillets
into 4 cm/1½ inch chunks and put into the soup with the pieces
of tomato and lemon rind. Before serving, toast the French
bread.

Work together the mayonnaise, crushed garlic and chilli flakes
to make the 'rouille' or sauce. Put a good teaspoon of this on
to each round of French bread.

Serve the soup in large warm bowls. Lower the rounds of
bread into the soup, and serve sprinkled well with parsley.

MINESTRONE

(serves 6 to 8)

In Italy this is traditionally served with freshly grated Parmesan cheese or a spoonful of pesto sauce. This sauce is also used with noodles and spaghetti. It is made from chopped fresh basil, crushed garlic, ground pine-nuts or walnuts and grated Parmesan, which are worked together with olive oil to make a smooth sauce.

Good fresh bread is obligatory!

2 large Spanish onions, peeled and chopped
2 cloves garlic, crushed
3 tblsp olive oil
1 tsp oregano
2 medium carrots, grated
3 sticks celery, finely chopped
2 400 g/14 oz tins chopped tomatoes
1.5 litres/2½ pints chicken or meat stock
100 g/4 oz small pasta shapes (bow or shell)
a wedge of green cabbage, roughly chopped
100 g/4 oz peas
100 g/4 oz French beans, chopped
1 tin borlotti beans, drained
sea salt and freshly ground black pepper

Soften the onions and garlic in the oil without browning them. Add the oregano, carrots and celery and continue to cook slowly for a few minutes. Now tip in the tomatoes (tinned tomatoes are excellent; they are sun ripened, which is more than can be said of the pallid, tasteless ones we import). Add the stock to the pan and bring to the boil. Put in the pasta and the cabbage and simmer for 10 minutes. Add the peas, French beans and borlotti beans, and simmer for another 3 or 4 minutes. Taste and season carefully.

Garnish with a handful of roughly chopped parsley if you have it. For a light meal this soup need only be followed with a pudding or fresh fruit.

Four
STARTERS

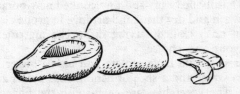

Starters are designed to whet the appetite for the main course but, even so, many of them can be quite rich. I have tried to give here recipes for only the most healthy starters but which still provide as much variety as possible. When planning your menus don't forget the importance of balance. For example, if you are having a cold dessert made primarily of fresh fruit, don't also choose to make a fresh fruit starter!

LES CRUDITÉS I

(serves 4)

The French often start a meal with 'crudités', which are an assortment of raw vegetables in colourful piles, dressed with a simple vinaigrette and served on individual plates. For example:

225 g/8 oz carrots, grated and sprinkled with a little orange juice
225 g/8 oz beetroot, cooked and diced
4 small ripe tomatoes, peeled, deseeded and sliced
½ small cucumber, thinly sliced
4 tblsp olive oil
2 tblsp lemon juice
snipped chives
sea salt and freshly ground pepper

Arrange the carrots, beetroot, tomatoes and cucumber attractively (in groups) on four individual plates. Sprinkle with olive oil, lemon juice, snipped chives and seasoning.

LES CRUDITÉS II
(serves 6–9)

A more elaborate version of Les Crudités is a collection of small raw vegetables and salads assembled in groups on a serving dish, with bowls of different sauces to accompany them.

Radishes, baby tomatoes, florets of cauliflower, sticks of celery and carrot, strips of sweet pepper, rounds of raw courgettes, endive leaves, baby beetroots (cooked), watercress sprigs, quartered hardboiled eggs and tiny cooked new potatoes are all suitable. Wash and dry them and arrange in groups in an attractive design on a chilled serving dish. The ingredients can be varied to your own choice.

Each guest should have a plate and also a finger bowl filled with warm water and a slice of lemon: rose petals add a touch of luxury. The vegetables are eaten with the fingers. Serve at least three sauces, in separate bowls; mustard sauce, garlic mayonnaise and anchovy sauce would be a good selection. Pass a basket of hot crusty bread, and sea salt and pepper mill.

AVOCADO PEAR SALAD
(serves 6)

This is how avocados are eaten in the West Indies.

3 avocado pears
juice of 1½ limes
1 lettuce, washed and shredded
sea salt and freshly ground black pepper
2 tsp Worcestershire sauce
2 limes for garnish

Halve, peel and slice the avocados lengthways. Sprinkle with lime juice and arrange on a bed of lettuce leaves. Tuck the avocado stones into the dish until the last minute (this prevents the pears from browning) and cover with clingfilm.

To serve, uncover, remove the stones and season with salt and freshly ground black pepper and dribble the Worcestershire sauce over the avocados. Garnish with wedges of lime.

MIKADO SALAD

(serves 6)

3 avocado pears
3 oranges
large bunch of watercress
50 g/2 oz chopped walnuts
yogurt dressing (see p. 189)

Peel and slice the avocados. Peel the oranges and separate into segments. Remove the membrane and pith from the segments.

Spoon the yogurt dressing on to each of six salad plates. Arrange the avocado slices and orange slices alternately in a fanlike pattern on the dressing. Put a generous clump of watercress in the centre of each and sprinkle with walnuts.

MELON WITH GINGER WINE

(serves 4)

1 small melon
4 oranges, segmented
4 tblsp ginger wine
1 egg white
castor sugar
4 sprigs mint

Scoop out the flesh from the melon with a small ball cutter. Place in a bowl with the orange segments (free from pith and membrane) and pour the ginger wine over. Cover and chill.

Dip the rims of four glasses first into lightly whisked egg white, then into castor sugar, to make a pretty frosting. To serve, turn the melon mixture into the prepared glasses and garnish each with a mint sprig.

AVOCADO AND CAVIAR MOUSSE

(serves 4)

1 avocado pear
juice of ½ lemon
2 spring onions
4 drops Tabasco
75 g/3 oz low-fat curd cheese
sea salt and freshly ground black pepper
58 g/2 oz Danish caviar

Halve the avocado and remove the flesh with a teaspoon. Put into a bowl with the lemon juice and stir in the spring onions and sieved cheese. Season to taste and gently fold in the caviar.

Serve on a plain white dish, surrounded by crisp lettuce leaves, with fingers of hot toast.

Note: This cannot be prepared too far ahead of the meal, or the avocado will lose its lovely colour.

COVENT GARDEN SALAD

(serves 4)

4 rashers lean bacon, rind removed
3 tomatoes, sliced
2 ripe avocado pears
1 small crisp lettuce

Dressing
1 tblsp cider vinegar
3 tblsp olive oil
½ tsp Dijon mustard
sea salt and freshly ground black pepper

Cook the rashers of bacon under the grill. Meanwhile, combine the ingredients for the dressing in a bowl. Peel the avocados carefully and slice into the dressing, turning the pieces gently until they are well coated.

Arrange the finely torn lettuce in individual china or glass bowls with the tomatoes. Spoon the avocado and dressing on to each and lastly snip the hot bacon over the top.

Serve immediately.

TZATZIKI

(serves 6)

This delicious Greek hors d'oeuvre can be served on its own, or for a bigger party it can be joined by bowls of taramasalata (smoked cod's roe pâté) and aubergine caviar. Serve with hot pitta bread.

½ medium cucumber
1 tsp sea salt
300 ml/½ pint low-fat yogurt
1 clove garlic, crushed
freshly ground pepper
1 tblsp chopped parsley (optional)

The cucumber can either be peeled and grated or finely diced for this recipe. Sprinkle with salt and drain in a colander for 30 minutes. Pat dry on absorbent paper and then combine with the remaining ingredients.

Keep in a cool place for an hour or so.

HUMMOUS

(serves 4–6)

450 g/1 lb tinned chick peas (preferably without sugar), drained
1 clove garlic, crushed
2 tblsp tahina paste
4 tblsp lemon juice
sea salt and pepper

Blend all this together and taste for seasoning. Sometimes I add a little finely chopped celery and peeled, chopped tomato. Garnish with a little paprika or chopped, fresh coriander leaves.

Hummous is a delicious and highly nutritious Middle Eastern food which is now widely popular in the West. It is good with wholemeal bread or as a dip for raw vegetables. It tastes wonderful as a dressing for salad and goes well with shish kebab. It is often served in Greek and Turkish restaurants with taramasalata (a pâté of smoked cod's roe) and tzatziki (yogurt, cucumber and mint).

It is perfect for packed lunches as it will pack and travel to work or school so safely.

TARAMASALATA

This creamy pâté of smoked cod's roe derives from Turkish and Greek kitchens. There it is more usual to use the roe of grey mullet. Tarama is a starter, a salad, a dip. It's what you want it to be and always delicious, to my mind.

100 g/4 oz smoked cod's roe
½ clove garlic, crushed
2 thick slices white bread
juice of 1 large lemon
3 tblsp olive oil
plenty of freshly ground white pepper
black olives to garnish

Take away any skin from the cod's roe and discard it. Mash the roe with a fork or a wooden spoon, adding the crushed garlic.

Remove the crusts from the bread and then soak the bread thoroughly in water. Squeeze it out and add it to the cod's roe and garlic. Now work everything well (using a pestle and mortar or blender or food processor – or just a bowl and wooden spoon and lots of elbow grease!).

Gradually incorporate the lemon juice and olive oil. Add plenty of pepper. Taste for enough lemon juice and pepper. Garnish simply with black olives.

Serve with warm pitta bread or wholemeal toast.

AUBERGINE PÂTÉ

5 medium aubergines
175 ml/6 fl oz olive oil
1 lemon
1 small onion
sea salt and lots of freshly ground black pepper

Prick the aubergines with a fork and bake them on a metal tray for 45 minutes in a preheated oven (190°C, Gas Mark 5, 375°F). Take off the skins when cool and liquidise the flesh, adding the oil slowly, then the lemon juice and seasoning. Turn into a dish. Chop the onion very finely and fold into the aubergine pâté by hand. Cover and leave the flavours to infuse for at least 4 hours.

Eat this delicious, simple pâté with chunks of fresh crusty bread.

FRESH TOMATO JUICE COCKTAIL

(serves 8)

A really refreshing starter. Make this when
tomatoes are plentiful.

1.75 kg/4 lb ripe tomatoes
1 tsp sugar
juice of 1 small lemon
good twist of lemon peel
2 tsp Worcestershire sauce
6–10 drops Tabasco sauce
1 tsp celery salt
freshly ground black pepper
lemon slices and finger-length sticks of celery to garnish

Roughly chop the tomatoes. Place in a liquidiser with the sugar. Blend and sieve. Pour the juice into a glass jug with the remaining ingredients and chill for several hours, for the lemon flavour to infuse.

Pour into individual glasses and garnish each with a lemon slice and a stick of celery.

YOGURT CHEESE WITH HERBS

(makes 100–175 g/4–6 oz)

600 ml/1 pint low-fat yogurt
sea salt and freshly ground white pepper
2 tblsp freshly chopped herbs (parsley, chervil and chives)

Line a sieve or a colander with muslin, empty the yogurt into it and place over a bowl. When it has drained for an hour or so, gather up the muslin ends and tie them into a knot. Hang this from a hook over the bowl, or from the taps in the kitchen sink, to drain overnight. Keep the liquid to use in soup.

Stir in salt and pepper and shape the cheese into a flattish round. Sprinkle the herbs on to a board and press the cheese on to them, first one side then the other. Sprinkle more herbs and then turn the cheese on them like a wheel, so that it is completely coated. Wrap in clingfilm and chill. Serve with butter curls and oat biscuits.

Note: This can also be made without the *fines herbes* when a plain yogurt cheese is preferred. If it is to accompany fruit, or to be used in sweet dishes, it should of course be unseasoned.

ARABIAN YOGURT APPETISER

(serves 4)

½ medium cucumber, diced
1 tsp sea salt
300 ml/½ pint low-fat yogurt
grated rind and juice of ½ lemon
100 g/4 oz seedless raisins
2 tblsp chopped walnuts
1 tblsp freshly chopped chives

Sprinkle the cucumber with salt and drain in a colander for about 30 minutes. Pat dry. Combine with the remaining ingredients and serve in small dishes. Provide teaspoons.

FRENCH BEANS AND
MUSHROOMS VINAIGRETTE

(serves 8)

75 g/3 oz blanched, halved almonds
a little olive oil to fry almonds
sea salt
1 kg/2 lb French beans
0.5 kg/1 lb button mushrooms
juice of ½ lemon
½ small onion, grated
a little ground coriander
3 tblsp chopped parsley
150 ml/scant ¼ pint French dressing (see p. 188).

Fry the almonds in oil, drain, then toss them in a little salt. Top and tail the beans and cook in boiling salted water until just tender, then cool under running water. Drain thoroughly.

Wipe the mushrooms with a clean damp cloth and slice finely. Sprinkle with lemon juice. Add the onion, coriander and parsley to the French dressing, then pour it over the mushrooms. Turn gently and leave for an hour or two.

Toss the mushroom mixture carefully with the French beans and serve in a simple china dish. Sprinkle the almonds on the top.

RADICCHIO, SPINACH AND CELERIAC SALAD

(serves 4)

1 head radicchio
50 g/2 oz young spinach leaves
150 g/5 oz celeriac, grated
150 g/5 oz carrot, grated
2 tblsp lemon juice
2 tblsp pumpkin seeds
sea salt and black pepper
3 tblsp sunflower oil
1 tsp runny honey

Wash the radicchio and spinach leaves. Toss the celeriac and carrot in lemon juice. Shred the radicchio and spinach into a chiffonnade (ribbons). Toast the pumpkin seeds by tossing them in a frying pan over a moderate heat for a few minutes. Mix the oil and honey with a little salt and pepper and toss the salad in it. Scatter with pumpkin seeds and serve.

VIRGIN ISLANDS SALAD

(serves 4)

1 lettuce
175 g/6 oz cottage cheese
2 tblsp chopped walnuts
2 bananas
2 tsp lime or lemon juice
150 ml/¼ pint low-fat yogurt
1 fresh mango

Wash the lettuce and arrange on four plates. Shape the cheese into balls about the size of a walnut and roll them in the chopped walnuts. Place the cheese balls on the lettuce leaves and add sliced bananas, sprinkled with lime or lemon juice. Top with the yogurt and sliced, peeled mango.

HERB CHEESE PÂTÉ

225 g/8 oz curd cheese
50 g/2 oz Stilton cheese
2 tblsp snipped chives
1 tblsp chopped parsley
1 tblsp chopped mint
sea salt and ground black pepper

Work the cheeses together in a bowl or food processor. Add the herbs and stir them in well. Season and taste.

Serve from a pretty dish or in individual ramekins. Garnish with fresh mint or parsley and, if you can, the flower heads of chives; they have pretty mauve mop heads.

MUSHROOMS EN COCOTTE

(*serves 4*)

0.5 kg/1 lb button mushrooms
1 tblsp sunflower oil
2 tblsp flour
300 ml/½ pint cider
2 tblsp fromage frais
sea salt and freshly ground black pepper
2 tblsp fresh breadcrumbs
1 tblsp chopped fresh herbs
parsley sprigs to garnish

Grease four individual ovenproof dishes. Sauté the mushrooms for a few minutes in the oil. Sprinkle the flour over and mix in gently. Add the cider slowly, mixing all together, and bring to the boil. Simmer for a few minutes and then stir in the fromage frais. Season to taste. Spoon into the ramekins and sprinkle over the breadcrumbs, mixed with chopped fresh herbs. Toast to golden brown under the grill. Serve garnished with parsley.

Five

LIGHT DISHES

These dishes are perfect for a light lunch or supper. Many of them can be served with fish or meat to make a more substantial meal. At the end of this section are also some ideas for sandwich fillings.

PASTA

The southern Italians are thought to enjoy one of the most healthy diets in Europe, and this is borne out by the low incidence of heart disease there. Pasta is one of their staple foods – along with plenty of olive oil. They place great emphasis on freshness (Italian housewives will shop twice a day for vegetables, salads and herbs). Pasta is made from wheat, Durum semolina and water mixed to a paste, shaped, and then dried slowly. It comes in a great variety of shapes and forms and is sometimes plain, sometimes green (spinach), or red (tomato), or made with eggs.

Cooking Packet (Dried) Pasta

Making fresh pasta requires space, patience and time – although, rather like bread making, it is a most satisfying job. But most Italians use dried pasta from a packet. Allow 50 g/2 oz per head for a starter and 100 g/4 oz per head for a main course. Cook it in plenty of boiling, salted water for about 10 minutes for large pasta, 7 minutes for the smaller types. Pasta must always be 'al dente', i.e. cooked until it is just done, soft but firm and never mushy. Drain thoroughly and put into a clean, hot dish and toss in a few spoonfuls of olive oil to stop it from sticking. Serve immediately, either plain like this (with the addition of pepper and grated Parmesan cheese) or with a sauce.

PASTA SHELLS WITH TOMATO, ANCHOVY AND GARLIC

(serves 6)

450 g/1lb pasta shells
3 tblsp olive oil
2 cloves of garlic, crushed
675 g/1½lb ripe tomatoes, peeled and chopped
1 small tin of anchovies
(fillets, first soaked in milk for about ½ hour)
a little sea salt and black pepper
grated Parmesan cheese to hand round separately

Boil the pasta shells in lots of boiling water, to which has been added a little sea salt and a dribble of oil, until just barely cooked and still a little firm. Drain, toss them in a little oil, and keep warm. Whilst the pasta is cooking heat the remaining olive oil and add the garlic. Cook for a minute or so without browning. Add the tomatoes, the chopped, drained anchovy fillets and a very little salt and some black pepper. Turn all this briefly over a good heat to heat right through.

Pour the tomato sauce over the pasta, toss well and serve with grated Parmesan.

SPAGHETTI WITH TOMATOES AND ROSEMARY

(serves 6)

575 g/20 oz spaghetti
2 tblsp olive oil
1 Spanish onion, chopped
2 tblsp finely chopped rosemary
2 cloves garlic, crushed
1 793 g/1lb 12 oz tin tomatoes
1 tblsp tomato purée
sea salt and freshly ground black pepper
½ tsp sugar
0.5 kg/1lb lean minced beef

Cook the spaghetti for 10 minutes in plenty of fast-boiling salted water. Drain, toss it in some olive oil and add plenty of freshly ground black pepper.

Meanwhile, cook the onions in the remaining oil until soft but not brown. Add the rosemary and garlic and fry gently for a little longer. Stir in the tomatoes, tomato purée, salt, pepper and sugar. Simmer, uncovered, for 10–15 minutes. Mix in the beef and stir until all the grains are separate. Bring gently back to the boil and simmer for 3 minutes only. Serve immediately, piled on the spaghetti.

Note: The beef *must* be good quality and freshly minced.

AUBERGINE CASSEROLE

(serves 6)

3–4 medium aubergines, sliced
sea salt and freshly ground black pepper
225 g/8 oz cottage cheese
a pinch of oregano
8 tomatoes, peeled and sliced
4 tblsp fresh breadcrumbs
1 clove garlic, chopped
olive oil

Sprinkle the aubergine slices with salt and leave to drain in a colander for about 1 hour. This removes any bitterness. Rinse and pat dry, then grill until golden brown on both sides.

Lightly oil a deep ovenproof dish, place a layer of aubergine slices in the bottom, season and cover with cottage cheese and oregano. Cover with a layer of tomato slices. Season again, lightly. Repeat the layers until the ingredients are used up, then top with the breadcrumbs mixed with the chopped garlic. Dribble a little olive oil over the breadcrumbs. Cook in a moderately hot oven (190°C, Gas Mark 5, 375°F) for 40–45 minutes.

TOPINAMBOURS PROVENÇALE

(serves 6)

1 kg/2 lb Jerusalem artichokes, scraped
2 large cloves garlic, crushed
1 tblsp olive oil
0.5 kg/1 lb tomatoes, peeled, deseeded and chopped
1 tblsp tomato purée
juice of ½ lemon
a little fresh thyme
1 tsp sugar
salt and freshly ground black pepper
2 tblsp chopped parsley

Slice the artichokes thickly and steam or poach until tender, about 20 minutes.

Meanwhile, warm the garlic in the oil, add the tomatoes and cook for about 10 minutes, stirring frequently, until the liquid has reduced a little. When the texture is pulpy, add the tomato purée, lemon juice, thyme, sugar and seasoning. Heat and pour it over the cooked artichokes in a serving dish. Just before serving sprinkle with chopped parsley. This is equally delicious hot or cold.

CHICKEN LIVERS WITH GRAPES

(serves 2)

This is quick and delicious.

100 g/¼ lb chicken livers, trimmed and chopped
25 g/1 oz butter
2 tsp flour
2 tblsp sherry or Madeira
3 tblsp low-fat yogurt
50 g/2 oz grapes, halved and pipped
sea salt and pepper

Heat a frying pan and quickly melt the butter in it, without burning. Tip in the chicken livers. Just turn them over the heat for a minute or two so that they are cooked on the outside and still pink within. Sprinkle the flour over and stir it all around. Now stir in the sherry (or Madeira). Cook very gently for 1 minute. Put in the grapes, season, taste and warm through. Eat it hot, served in ramekins, with wholemeal bread and a salad.

Note: The sauce with the chicken livers should be about as thick as cream.

STUFFED TOMATOES

(serves 6)

6 medium mushrooms
1 shallot or small onion
1 stick celery
1 tblsp olive oil
2 tsp chopped basil
1 tblsp chopped parsley
4 tblsp fresh white breadcrumbs
sea salt and freshly ground black pepper
6 large, firm tomatoes
6 rounds toast
1 small clove garlic, crushed
parsley sprigs to garnish

Clean and peel the mushrooms and remove stalks. Chop peelings and stalks finely and keep on one side. Finely chop the shallot and celery. Heat half the oil and cook the shallot and celery very slowly. Add the mushroom peelings and stalks and continue to cook over a low heat until everything is soft (about 7 minutes). Add the herbs and breadcrumbs and continue cooking, turning everything about in the pan, until the breadcrumbs have begun to brown. Season to taste.

Cut the tops off the tomatoes and scoop out the seeds and juice; drain the tomatoes upside down for a minute. Fry the mushroom caps in the remaining oil. Stuff the tomatoes with the breadcrumb mixture and top each with a fried mushroom cap. Place the tomatoes on rounds of toasted bread stamped out with a cutter or a glass and rubbed with garlic. Cover with greased foil and bake in a hot oven (220°C, Gas Mark 7, 425°F) for 10 minutes. Garnish with parsley.

STUFFED GREEN PEPPERS

(serves 6)

6 green peppers
100 g/4 oz long-grain rice
grated rind and juice of 1 large lemon
3 tblsp chopped herbs (parsley, chives and thyme)
2 tblsp grated carrot
1 tblsp sultanas
150 ml/¼ pint French dressing
made with 6 tblsp olive oil,
the lemon juice,
½ tsp each sugar,
sea salt and pepper (see p. 16).

Slice lids off the peppers and carefully remove all seeds and pith from inside. Wash, blanch for 6 minutes in boiling water, then plunge immediately into cold water, to keep the colour fresh. Drain and pat dry with kitchen paper.

Boil the rice in plenty of salted water for 10 minutes. Drain and cool. Flavour the rice with the grated lemon rind and chopped herbs. Combine with the grated carrot and sultanas. Toss with French dressing and pile into the peppers. Replace the pepper lids. Finally pour a little French dressing over the peppers and serve.

PIZZA QUICHE

(serves 6)

This is very good, and contains no eggs. The black olives and red tomatoes look very effective together.

175 g/6 oz easy-mix pastry with oil (see p. 206)
1 56 g/2 oz can anchovy fillets
2 large Spanish onions, chopped
3 tblsp olive oil
6 large ripe tomatoes, peeled and chopped
sea salt and freshly ground black pepper
pinch sugar
1 tblsp tomato purée
1 tsp dried oregano
1 tsp capers
black olives
olive oil to sprinkle

Line a 20 cm/8 inch flan tin with the pastry and bake blind in a moderately hot oven (200°C, Gas Mark 6, 400°F) for 15 minutes.

Halve the anchovy fillets lengthways and soak in milk.

Cook the onions in the oil until soft but not brown, then add the chopped tomatoes, seasoning, sugar, tomato purée and oregano. Cook gently for about 5 minutes, mashing the tomatoes slightly with a wooden spoon. Turn into the prepared pastry case, spreading evenly. Drain the anchovies and arrange in a lattice pattern over the tomato mixture, then sprinkle with drained, rinsed capers. Put one black olive in each of the squares and sprinkle with a little oil. Bake in a moderately hot oven (180°C, Gas Mark 4, 350°F) for about 20 minutes.

SPINACH QUICHE

(serves 8)

100 g/4 oz flour
100 g/4 oz White Flora
or 50 g/2 oz White Flora and 50 g/2 oz butter
100 g/4 oz roast hazelnuts, ground
¼ tsp sea salt
1 tsp chopped fresh thyme
2 tblsp skimmed milk

Filling
4–5 spring onions
25 g/1 oz butter
1 tblsp flour
225 g/8 oz chopped cooked spinach
sea salt and freshly ground pepper
225 g/8 oz cottage cheese
pinch grated nutmeg
2 tblsp grated Parmesan cheese
2 egg whites

Make the pastry following the method for basic shortcrust (see p. 205), adding the ground hazelnuts, salt and thyme with the remaining flour, and substituting skimmed milk for the water. Line a 25 cm/10 inch flan tin with the pastry, cover with grease-proof paper and fill with baking beans. Bake blind for 15 minutes in a moderately hot oven (200°C, Gas Mark 6, 400°F).

Meanwhile, finely chop the spring onions, discarding the green parts. Fry in the butter until softened. Add, and stir in the flour. Drain the spinach thoroughly and add the onions. Cook for a few minutes, stirring. Season well and add the cottage cheese, nutmeg and Parmesan cheese. Fold in the stiffly whisked egg whites and pile into the pastry shell. Return to the oven and bake at 190°C, Gas Mark 5, 375°F for 30 minutes.

HAZELNUT AND LEEK QUICHE

(serves 8)

Pastry
100 g/4 oz flour
100 g/4 oz White Flora
or 50 g/2 oz White Flora and 50 g/2 oz butter
100 g/4 oz roast hazelnuts, ground
½ tsp sea salt
½ tsp chopped marjoram
2 tblsp skimmed milk

Filling
4 large leeks
25 g/1 oz butter
2 tblsp flour
300 ml/½ pint skimmed milk
3 tblsp grated low-fat cheese (Edam or Gouda)
2 tblsp grated Parmesan cheese
sea salt and freshly ground black pepper
4 tblsp fresh breadcrumbs
1 tsp chopped fresh thyme or marjoram
sunflower oil to sprinkle

Make the pastry, use to line a 25cm/10 inch flan tin and bake blind, all as for spinach quiche.

Chop the white part of the leeks, wash and clean thoroughly. Cook for about 10 minutes in boiling, salted water. Drain well.

Melt the butter, stir the flour into it and cook for 1 minute. Gradually add the milk and bring to the boil, stirring all the time. Stir the cheeses in and season to taste. Fold the leeks into the cheese sauce and pour into the prepared pastry case. Mix the breadcrumbs with the thyme and use to top the quiche. Sprinkle a little oil over. Bake in a moderately hot oven (190°C, Gas Mark 5, 375°F) for 30 minutes.

VEGETABLE AND TOFU CASSEROLE

(serves 3–4)

Speedily made and nourishing, this is an ideal meal in a pot that needs no more accompaniment than a hunk of bread. Tofu can be bought in health food shops. It is a vegetable product, made from bean curd. It is a rich source of protein. Try it if you never have before.

2 tblsp sunflower oil
2 large onions, peeled and sliced
1 large green pepper, deseeded
450 g/1 lb tomatoes, peeled and quartered
4 tblsp yogurt (optional)
100 g/4 oz tofu, cut into squares the size of sugar cubes
sea salt and black pepper

Cook the onions gently in the oil until they begin to soften. Chop the pepper and cook it with the onions for another 5 minutes or so. Stir into them the tomatoes, then cover and simmer gently for about 20 minutes. Add the cubed tofu and heat through. Serve in hot soup bowls with bread and butter.

PERFECT PANCAKES

A good pan should ideally be kept solely for the purpose of making pancakes. Choose non-stick or one with a good stout base. If it is *not* non-stick 'seal' it first like this: make the pan very hot with a little salt in it and then give it a quick rub with kitchen paper. Toss away the salt. Make the empty pan hot again, add a few spoonfuls of olive oil and heat until it is nearly smoking, then wipe out again with dry kitchen paper. The pan is now 'sealed' and should not need washing after this – try to keep it clean from now on by simply wiping. Store it with a piece of paper on its surface to stop it being scratched by something else in the pot cupboard.

Basic pancake batter

Pancake batter should be left to stand for about half an hour to let the starch swell – this will make your pancakes lighter.

100 g/4 oz flour
pinch of salt
1 large egg
300 ml/½ pint milk
sunflower oil

Sift the flour into a bowl (or put into a blender), adding the salt.

Mix together the egg and the milk with a tablespoon of oil (or add to the blender goblet, blending briefly). Make a well in the flour and mix in the liquid ingredients, drawing in the flour gradually until the batter is quite smooth and about the thickness of single cream. Set aside for half an hour.

Set the pancake pan on the heat. Meanwhile check that the batter has not become too thick and if it has, add a little more milk. Wipe a little oil around the pan with a brush (or a piece of crumpled greaseproof paper). Now for the good bit. Pour in just enough batter to coat the base of your pan right to its edges by swirling the pan about a bit. Cook over the heat until the pancake edges are curling up and tiny bubbles start to appear – about a minute over a moderate heat. Flip it over with a palette knife and cook until the underneath turns golden. Now I don't know if I should tell you this but my first pancake is always a failure and I have to eat it myself. So if it breaks as you try to turn it over, just enjoy it.

Continue cooking the pancakes like this – but without either breaking them or eating them – until the batter is all used up. After a little practice you can try tossing them and dispense with the palette knife except for using it to lift up the edges so you can peep underneath to see if they are done.

Oil the pan lightly between each pancake.

Variations to basic batter

- Half the milk can be replaced with beer.
- Half the flour can be replaced with buckwheat flour for blinis, which are eaten with pretend caviar and low-fat yogurt by people on a low-cholesterol diet and an economy drive!
- Chopped chives can be added, or ¼ tsp caraway seeds.
- Chickpea pancakes make a change. Simply use chickpea flour instead of white flour. They can be spicy with the addition of a few grilled, ground cumin seeds, chilli flakes (go easy), a little turmeric or ¼ tsp garam masala. Make these pancakes a bit thicker and replace half the milk with water. Use more oil in the pan.
- For sweet pancakes include 1 tsp sugar and you may be moved to add a pinch of cinnamon or nutmeg too.

VEGETABLE FILLINGS FOR PANCAKES

(these serve 6)

Carrot filling
2 tblsp oil or butter
2 tblsp finely chopped shallots
6 carrots, diced small
300 ml/½ pint chicken stock
½ tsp ground coriander
1 tsp sugar
sea salt and pepper to taste
2 tblsp fromage frais
1 tblsp chopped parsley

Soften the shallots in oil for a few minutes. Add the chicken stock, carrots, coriander, sugar, salt and pepper and cook until the carrots are tender and the liquid nearly evaporated. Transfer into the bowl of a food processor or the goblet of a blender and whizz till smooth, gradually adding the fromage frais. If you prefer a slightly less than smooth texture, just use a potato masher. Stir in the chopped parsley.

Spinach filling
2 tblsp oil or butter
2 tblsp finely chopped shallots
225 g/½ lb cooked spinach (squeezed well dry)
1 tblsp Pernod
a little grated nutmeg
sea salt and pepper to taste
3 tblsp fromage frais

Soften the shallots in oil as above. Add the spinach, Pernod, nutmeg, salt and pepper and fromage frais. Stir together and heat through before filling the pancakes.

Mushroom filling
2 tblsp oil or butter
2 tblsp finely chopped shallots
350 g/¾ lb mushrooms, sliced
2 tsp lemon juice
a little chopped lemon thyme
2 tblsp fromage frais
sea salt and pepper to taste

Soften the shallots as above. Add the sliced mushrooms, lemon juice, thyme and salt and pepper and cook briefly until the mushrooms are tender. Stir the fromage frais into the vegetables.

To assemble: Divide the fillings between the pancakes evenly, placing the filling in the middle and folding in the sides to make a parcel. Place them side by side in a warm heatproof dish and put them in the oven to warm through (but do not allow them to dry out).

They can be dusted with grated Parmesan cheese or finely chopped nuts, or served with a sauce – or just a blob of yogurt.

BOSTON BAKED BEANS

(serves 4–6)

100 g/4 oz pea or navy beans (small white beans)
350 g/12 oz lean salt pork
1 tblsp sea salt
3 tblsp sugar
1 tblsp to 1 cup molasses (according to taste)
½ tsp mustard
boiling water

Pick over beans, cover with cold water, and soak overnight. Drain, cover with fresh water, heat slowly (water below boiling point), and cook until skins will burst – which is best determined by taking a few beans on the tip of a spoon and blowing on them. Drain beans. Scald pork and scrape, remove ¼ inch slice, and put in bottom of bean pot. Score rind of remaining pork every 1.25 cm/½ inch, making cuts 2.5 cm/1 inch deep. Put beans in pot and bury pork in beans, leaving rind exposed. Mix salt, molasses and sugar, add one cup boiling water to cover beans. Cover bean pot and bake 6 to 8 hours in slow oven, 120°C, Gas Mark ½, 250°F, uncovering for the last hour of cooking so that the rind may become brown and crisp. Add water as needed.

Baked kidney beans: cook as for Boston baked beans.

Boston beans, New York style: omit molasses. Bake in a shallow pan. Arrange slices of salt pork over top. Do not add water during last hour of cooking.

BEAN SPROUTS
WITH MUSHROOMS AND HAM
(serves 4)

1 leek, white part only
175 g/6 oz mushrooms
2 tblsp sunflower oil
450 g/1 lb bean sprouts
150 ml/¼ pint water
1 tblsp sherry
100 g/4 oz cooked ham, chopped
2 tblsp cornflour
1 tblsp soy sauce
1 tblsp lemon juice

Slice the leek and mushrooms and sauté them in oil for 5 minutes. Add the bean sprouts and continue cooking until they are a light golden colour. Add the water and sherry and simmer for 5 minutes. Now add the ham.

Combine the cornflour, soy sauce and water to make a paste. Stir this into the simmering vegetables and cook for 1 minute more until thickened. Serve warm or at room temperature with chunks of French bread or a bowl of brown rice.

RICE PILAF
(serves 4)

225 g/8 oz long-grain rice
1 onion, chopped
2 tblsp olive oil
1 tsp ground turmeric
1 tblsp currants
1 (113 g/4 oz) can pineapple pieces, drained
fresh coriander leaves

Cook the rice in boiling salted water for 10 minutes. Drain and sprinkle with a little cold water to separate the grains. Keep warm in a covered dish.

Fry the onion in the oil, add the turmeric, currants and pineapple pieces. Toss the rice in the mixture and serve garnished with fresh coriander leaves.

LITTLE LOAVES AND FISHES

(serves 2)

2 small French loaves
2 tins sardines
2 tomatoes, peeled, depipped and chopped fine
1 lemon
chilli flakes and seasoning

Split open the loaves without separating the two halves.

Mash together the drained sardines, tomatoes, juice of lemon, chilli flakes (just a very little) and seasoning.

Fill the loaves with the mixture, close them and wrap in foil.

These are very good served as they are or heated in their foil over a barbeque fire.

PAN BAGNA

Pan bagna is as familiar on the south coast of France as a ham sandwich is here. Usually made with a baguette (French loaf), it is a vehicle for anyone's favourite things.

1 stubby French loaf
3 tblsp French dressing
1 clove garlic, crushed
heart of lettuce
3 ripe tomatoes, sliced
1 small onion, skinned and sliced and soaked in cold water
1 small red pepper, deseeded and sliced
1 small tin of tuna fish in brine, drained
2 tblsp pitted black olives
sea salt and freshly ground black pepper

Split the loaf in half lengthways without quite separating the two halves. Mix the French dressing with the crushed garlic and sprinkle this inside the bread. Lay the lettuce leaves on the bottom half and place the remaining ingredients along the top. Season with sea salt and lots of freshly ground black pepper.

Cover all this by pressing down the top half of the loaf. Wrap in clingfilm or foil.

It is best not eaten for an hour or so because this gives the flavours time to mingle. The oils and juices get absorbed into the bread.

Unwrap and cut into slices.

ANCHOVY BREAD

1 French stick
1 tin anchovies
1 clove garlic
pepper (no salt)
olive oil

Heat the oven to 200°C, Gas Mark 6, 400°F.

Cut the bread lengthways. Work the anchovies, garlic, pepper and oil with a pestle and mortar, using lots of oil.

Spread on the cut side of the bread. Before serving heat the bread in the oven (or under the grill).

Serve with rough red wine – ideally in the sun, listening to the sea.

TAPÉNADE

(serves)

This is a Provençal sauce. Serve it with cold meat like beef or lamb – or with cold fish, beans or tuna fish.

1 small tin of anchovy fillets, rinsed in milk or water
100 g/4 oz stoned black olives, rinsed and chopped
2 tsp mustard (Dijon if possible)
juice of 1 lemon
plenty of black pepper
175 g/6 oz capers, drained and rinsed
50 g/2 oz tuna fish (optional)
150 ml/¼ pint olive oil

Pound the anchovies, olives, mustard, lemon juice, capers and tuna using a pestle and mortar or blend in a liquidiser or food processor, adding the olive oil a little at a time as you would for mayonnaise.

This mixture keeps well in a jar in the fridge.

For a picnic, sprinkle a cut loaf of French bread with a little olive oil and spread with tapénade. Fill with lettuce and tomato and cover with the other half of the loaf.

Salade Niçoise is another favourite recipe, found in restaurants everywhere now, and tapénade sauce (from the local south of France name for a caper) can also be used as a spread on French bread: lovely for a picnic or starter snack. The tomato and onion tart called pissaladière is a similar sort of food; it's the Provençal version of a pizza.

SEND FOR A SANDWICH

The Earl of Sandwich called for slices of cold roast beef between two pieces of buttered bread so that he need not leave the gaming table and interrupt his sport.

It's hard to believe that no one had thought of this simple device before – but there you are. Anyway, it certainly caught on and nowadays provides many of us with our midday meal. Its neat and convenient form and its flexibility make it quite invaluable to most of us.

If the sandwich is actually a meal (and not just a snack) it is important to make sure that both the bread and its filling are really nutritious. The bread should be fresh and tempting and preferably wholemeal – sliced if you are making large quantities of sandwiches – or choose one of a variety of different types and grains, such as soda bread or yeast, rolls, baps or baguettes.

Spread the bread with butter (remember to leave it out of the fridge overnight) or a good margarine that is high in polyunsaturates. The American sandwich is always spread with a smear of mayonnaise. Butters can be specially blended before spreading, with chopped herbs, a squeeze of lemon, a little mustard or horseradish – or anything that seems appropriate to the chosen filling. Most sandwiches that are savoury are improved by the addition of a little shredded salad such as lettuce leaves, sprouting seeds or beans, or watercress.

The more ingredients that can be persuaded to stay between the slices of bread, the better. When I was a child there was a cartoon character called Dagwood who crept into the kitchen at night to raid the fridge to make gigantic triple-deckers for himself. At the exact moment that his mouth opened wide for the first wonderful bite, his nagging little wife Blondie would enter to scream at him.

A large sliced loaf makes enough sandwiches for 4 for an informal lunch or supper. So for 20 people allow 5 large sliced loaves. This is just a rough guide. About 675g (1½lb) of butter will do these 5 loaves.

Four different sandwich varieties will be enough, and it is nice to include one sweet one, like banana and walnut and honey, to eat for 'pudding'.

Here are some suggestions for this type of 'do'.

- bacon/tomato/lettuce
- tuna fish/green olives/mayonnaise/lettuce

- sliced cucumber dressed with a little French dressing
- banana/honey/date

- egg/butter/mustard and cress
- chicken/lettuce/black grapes
- avocado/tomato/lettuce
- peanut butter/redcurrant jelly

- avocado/mayonnaise/prawn/lettuce
- chopped ham/chutney/grated cheddar-type cheese
- cottage cheese/chopped dill/pickled cucumbers/diced celery
- roast beef/shredded lettuce/horseradish cream

Arrange the sandwiches on big dishes or small trays covered with foil. I always serve them trimmed of crusts but it is certainly more economical to leave them on. Scatter the sandwiches with plenty of mustard and cress or a little shredded lettuce to keep them fresh-looking. Label each dish with an identifying card and then cover carefully with clingfilm.

Here is a list of sandwich filling suggestions so that you will never be stuck for ideas for the children's lunch boxes or for picnics.

Sandwich Filling Ideas

All made with wholemeal bread:

banana/date
banana/fig
banana/walnut/date
banana/honey/date/peanut butter
banana/honey/date/fig
banana/peanut butter

Marmite/cucumber
Marmite/mustard and cress
Marmite/salad
hummous/lettuce
hummous/celery
tomato/chopped fresh basil
tomato/spring onion/lettuce
sprouting seeds*/avocado/salad

*See note overleaf.

tofu pâté/chopped celery/chopped sweet red pepper
tofu pâté/mustard and cress

cottage cheese/honey/banana
cottage cheese/walnut/date
cottage cheese/pitted black olives/chopped parsley
cottage cheese/honey/date/banana/fig
cottage cheese/date/apple
cottage cheese/sliced dried apricot
cottage cheese/date/pineapple
cottage cheese/sprouting seeds*/Marmite
low-fat curd cheese/celery/salad
low-fat curd cheese/walnut/date
low-fat curd cheese/avocado/salad
low-fat curd cheese/salad/chopped gherkins
low-fat curd cheese/tomato/sprouting seeds*

taramasalata/cucumber
taramasalata/salad/yogurt
tuna/sweetcorn/lettuce/mayonnaise
tuna/cucumber/chopped green olives
tuna/sprouting seeds*/chopped parsley
sardines/lemon chips/pinch chilli flakes
sardines/tomato/lettuce

chicken/grapes/chopped celery
chicken/sweetcorn/lettuce
chicken/mustard and cress/mayonnaise
chicken/avocado/salad
turkey/coleslaw/salad
turkey/black grapes/salad
turkey/sprouting seeds*/banana
pheasant/celery/apple

ham/gherkins/mustard
ham/salad/mustard
ham/mustard and cress/pickle or chutney
ham/tomato/mustard
lean roast beef/horseradish/lettuce
lean roast beef/walnuts/mustard

---

*Sprouting seeds and beans are sold in health food shops. They contain a mixture such as chick peas, aduki beans, brown lentils, puy lentils and mung beans.

Six
FISH

Fish is delicious, nutritious and economical. It used to be a cheap dish – but nothing is cheap now. So we can only look to buy *good* food that gives value for money.

Fish is rich in protein and minerals, easily digested and low in harmful fats. It has the advantage of being quick and easy to cook. It is simply the most marvellous food for young and old.

People who don't like fish have probably never had it properly prepared, or possibly had fish that was less than fresh. (Or maybe both.) It is important to make friends with a first-class fishmonger or find a good market, then the fish should be prepared and eaten the same day.

It is a good idea to prepare too much for the meal as it is wonderful to have cold the next day for a salad at lunchtime.

SMOKED FISH

Good Scotch smoked salmon is always wonderful and a great compliment to your guests, but as it is very expensive it is worth experimenting with some of the other varieties of smoked fish. Smoked trout is served with horseradish sauce. Smoked mackerel and buckling are good too, and cheaper. Smoked eels are some people's passion – but they are very much a matter of personal taste.

Serve smoked fish as a starter or lunch dish with a selection of the following: brown bread and butter, lemon wedges, horseradish sauce and lettuce hearts.

SMOKED MACKEREL PÂTÉ

(serves 4)

This is a no-fuss supper party recipe. If there is any left over it will make a lovely filling for brown bread sandwiches.

225 g/8 oz smoked mackerel fillets
juice of 1 lemon
75 ml/⅛ pint low-fat yogurt
freshly ground black pepper
50 g/2 oz fromage frais

Garnish
slices of lemon
sprigs of parsley

Remove the skin from the smoked fillets. Flake the fish into a food processor or blender. Add the lemon juice, yogurt and black pepper. Blend these ingredients until smooth and then quickly blend in the fromage frais. Heap into a dish and smooth over the top.

Garnish the pâté with lemon slices and parsley sprigs and place in the refrigerator to set.

CAVEACHED SALMON

(serves 6)

The old Mexican word for 'cooking' fish in lemon and lime juice, rather than with heat, is *ceviche* – which is not far from the Elizabethan word *caveach*. So presumably one or other country introduced it to the other. Recipe swapping is nothing new!

225 g/8 oz very fresh cod, skinned and cut into 2.5 cm/1 inch cubes
225 g/8 oz salmon, skinned and cut into 1 inch cubes
juice of 2 lemons or 4 limes
4 tblsp olive oil
4 tblsp chopped parsley and chives
1 tsp chopped marjoram (or a pinch of dried oregano)
4 ripe tomatoes, skinned, deseeded and chopped
1 small green or red sweet pepper, deseeded and finely chopped
sea salt and freshly ground black pepper
6 olives, pipped and finely chopped
2 avocados, peeled and cubed
2 lemons or limes for garnishing
6 good lettuce leaves

Put the cubed fish in a glass bowl. Check it for bones. Pour the lemon or lime juice over it and leave to marinate for at least 6 hours.

Combine olive oil, herbs, tomatoes, green pepper, olives and seasoning. Tip away some of the juice from the fish if there is a lot. Mix the fish with the oil and herb mixture and marinate for another hour. Peel and cube the avocados and fold them in.

To serve, put a wedge of lemon (or lime) on the side and a lettuce leaf in the centre of each plate. Use the lettuce as a cup and fill it with the caveach.

MEDITERRANEAN FISH
(À DEUX)

(*serves 2*)

A light no-fuss supper dish.

2 tblsp olive oil
1 Spanish onion, finely chopped
1 clove garlic, crushed
4 tomatoes, peeled and chopped
275 g/10 oz fillets of any white fish
(plaice, cod or haddock)
sea salt and freshly ground black pepper
juice of 1 lemon
parsley, chopped

Sauté the onion and garlic in oil until soft and golden. Add the tomatoes. Pour half this mixture into an ovenproof dish. Place the seasoned fillets on the top, cover with the remaining tomato and onion sauce. Add the juice of the lemon, cover the dish and cook, until the fish is done, on top of the cooker or in a moderate oven (190°C, Gas Mark 5, 375°F) for about 25 minutes. Dust with parsley.

GRAVAD LAX

(serves 8)

This is my Norwegian mother-in-law's recipe for home-cured salmon, which in Norway is considered more of a delicacy than smoked salmon. If you are economising, buy the tailpiece of the salmon and negotiate a good price with your fishmonger. A fresh mackerel is also excellent treated in the same way, head removed and filleted.

1 kg/2 lb piece of salmon, or 1 large mackerel
juice of 1 small lemon

For the mixture
4 tblsp sea salt
6 tblsp castor sugar
2 tblsp crushed black peppercorns
3 tblsp chopped dill weed

Mix together the ingredients for the mixture. Lay a large piece of clingfilm or foil on a plate and spread on a quarter of this mixture, to an area the size of the fish. Over it lay the opened-out fish, skin side down. Remove any remaining fish bones, then spread half the mixture over the fish. Fold to make a fish shape again, and spread the remaining quarter of the mixture on top. Close up the clingfilm or foil and seal to make a neat parcel. Place on a board and cover with a weight.

Leave in the refrigerator for 3–4 days, turning the parcel twice a day. Unwrap and drain. I usually scrape off some of the 'cure' before slicing the salmon. Slice the salmon in the same way as smoked salmon, but don't worry too much about getting it very fine. Sprinkle with the lemon juice.

Serve with brown bread and butter and a slightly sweet sauce that complements it perfectly.

Make the sauce by melting a tablespoon of brown sugar in a little brandy or lemon juice, adding 2 teaspoons of Dijon mustard, and stirring this into a cup of mayonnaise. Add a teaspoon of chopped dill and leave for a few hours for the flavours to marry.

Note: The salmon freezes well. Drain thoroughly and wrap in fresh clingfilm.

COD WITH TOMATOES

(serves 4)

Baking in the oven like this is a method very well suited to fish; it cooks gently and retains all the lovely juices. Variations on this recipe are to be found on Cyprus, in Greece and all along the Mediterranean shores.

1 Spanish onion, chopped
3 tblsp olive oil
½ tsp fennel or coriander seeds
675 g/1½ lb ripe tomatoes, skinned and chopped
juice of 1 lemon
sea salt and freshly ground black pepper
4 good-sized cod steaks

Soften the onion in oil until it is transparent. Add the crushed fennel or coriander and then the tomatoes. Spoon a third of the mixture into the base of an ovenproof dish. Lay the cod steaks on top and season them with the lemon juice and a little sea salt and pepper.

Cover the fish with the remainder of the onion and tomato, then season lightly again. Cover loosely with a piece of foil. Bake in a moderate hot oven (190°C, Gas Mark 5, 375°F) for about 25 minutes or until the fish is barely cooked.

COD WITH MUSTARD AND TOMATOES

Cod is one of the finest fish that money can buy. It is, at its freshest, firm and white with flakes of delicious essence of the sea. Mustard might seem a strange companion to fish but it really is most awfully good. Use a Dijon or a fairly mild smooth mustard. This is excellent with coley too.

Squeeze a little lemon juice into ¼ cup of water and pour it into an ovenproof dish. Brush fillets of cod (or coley) with a little oil, spread with a smear of mustard and put them in the dish. Lay slices of tomato on the top and season lightly. Cook in a moderate oven (190°C, Gas Mark 5, 375°F) until barely cooked – about 10–15 minutes.

Alternatively the fish can be cooked under the grill. Cook with the skin side upwards first. Pull the skin off and discard it. Turn the fillets and smear with the mustard, lay the tomato slices on top, season and grill until done.

Serve with plain boiled potatoes and a salad.

MRS MULLER'S FISH MOUSSE
(serves 4–6)

This is a recipe from an old friend in Trinidad. It is good made with any fresh white fish such as cod.

She says: 'Simmer a bouquet garni for ¼ hour and then add a cod's head and backbone and cook for a further ten minutes. When cooked and cooled, strain liquor. Here are the proportions for the mousse:

300 ml/½ pint fish liquid
2 tsp gelatine, dissolved in fish liquid
600 ml/1 pint cooked fish, skinned, boned and flaked
150 ml/¼ pint mayonnaise (see p. 192)
150 ml/¼ pint fromage frais
2 tblsp chopped chives
seasoning
1 egg white, stiffly whipped

Stir all but the egg white together and then fold that in. Set in a wetted mould. Turn out and serve garnished with the lettuce hearts.'

MONKFISH SKEWERS
(serves 4)

450 g/1 lb monkfish
1 red pepper
175 g/6 oz button mushrooms
4 tomatoes, halved
1 banana, sliced into 8
olive oil
juice of 1 lemon
salt and freshly ground black pepper

Cut the monkfish into chunks, removing skin and bones. Remove the pith and pips from the red pepper, cut it into chunks and blanch them in boiling water for a few minutes. Drain.

Put the fish, pepper, mushrooms, tomatoes and banana into the oil and lemon juice. Season and turn until all is shiny and evenly coated with the dressing.

Now thread on to skewers, alternating the ingredients until they are all used up.

Grill, turning and basting occasionally with the oil and lemon, for 8–10 minutes under a gentle to medium heat.

Arrange on a bed of shredded lettuce with chunks of lemon. Serve with boiled, plain or saffron, rice; watercress and orange salad goes well with this.

LEMON SOLE WITH MUSHROOMS AND CIDER

(serves 4)

8 lemon sole fillets, skinned
sea salt and white pepper
450 ml/¾ pint dry cider
0.5 kg/1 lb button mushrooms
1 tblsp sunflower oil
3 tblsp flour
450 g/1 lb potatoes, cooked
parsley sprig to garnish

Season the sole fillets with salt and pepper, fold each into three and lay in a sauté pan. Pour in the cider. Bring slowly to the boil. Cover and cook for a few minutes over a gentle heat.

Meanwhile, slice the mushrooms and cook in the oil until just soft. Sprinkle the flour on to the mushrooms and mix in carefully, until absorbed. Strain the cider liquor from the fish into a bowl and then add slowly to the mushrooms, stirring. Cook for a few minutes, stirring all the time, until the sauce thickens.

Arrange the sole fillets on a hot serving dish and pour the mushroom and cider sauce over them. Cream the potatoes with skimmed milk, season, and pipe a border around the fish. Garnish with a sprig of parsley and serve with a mixed green salad.

DOVER SOLE VERONIQUE

(serves 2)

1 fish per person
lemon juice
white grapes, stoned
capers
sunflower oil
seasoning

Mornay sauce
See recipe for white sauce (p. 195)
Make half the quantity and add 25 g/1 oz grated
cheese when it begins to bubble

Buy the sole on the bone and ask your fishmonger to skin and slit them down the backbone and make pockets for stuffing.

Wash and dry the fish. Squeeze lemon juice into the pockets. Now put a stoned white grape with a caper in it into each pocket.

Brush the fish with oil and season lightly.

Cook for 20 minutes in a moderately hot oven (190°C, Gas Mark 5, 375°F) or until the sole is just cooked through.

Meanwhile make the mornay sauce.

When fish is cooked, pour a little sauce over each fish and brown gently under the grill.

FISH IN A BRICK
(serves 2)

One of the Venetian ways of preparing fish is to bake it in earthenware in the oven, with oil and herbs and lemon, and then to serve it cold, with more oil, herbs and lemon. Mackerel, red mullet or grey mullet are suitable fish for cooking in this way.

1 large fish, cleaned
2 tblsp olive oil
1 bay leaf, crumbled
2 tsp finely chopped thyme or fennel
1 lemon, sliced
sea salt and freshly ground black pepper

First soak a fish brick in cold water for 10 minutes. Remove.

Make a few incisions in the uppermost side of the fish. Mix together the oil, herbs, lemon slices and seasoning. Sprinkle half this mixture inside the fish and over the cuts. Rub the underside with a little extra oil. Lay the fish in the brick and replace the cover. Put the brick into a cold oven and set to 190°C, Gas Mark 5, 375°F. Cook for about 1 hour. Allow to cool and serve with the remaining oil and herb mixture poured over.

Potato salad and tomato salad would accompany this well.

Note: If you do not have a fish brick, instead wrap the fish in foil and place in a roasting tin.

HAKE PROVENÇALE

(*serves* 6)

1.25 kg/3 lb hake in one piece
450 g/1 lb onions, finely chopped
1 clove garlic, crushed
675 g–1 kg/1½–2 lb tomatoes, skinned, deseeded
and roughly chopped
olive oil
butter
sea salt and freshly ground black pepper

Skin the fish and wash it well under running cold water. Gently cook the onions, garlic and tomato in a little olive oil in a covered pan, seasoning with sea salt and pepper, until they are quite soft.

Put the fish in a baking pan just large enough to hold it, and spread the onion and tomato mixture all over it. Add a few small knobs of butter, cover the pan well with a buttered grease-proof paper and cook in a fairly hot oven (200°C, Gas Mark 6, 400°F) for about 50 minutes, until the fish is cooked right through.

Remove to a serving dish, being careful not to disturb the coating of vegetable mixture. Reduce the cooking liquid a little and pour it over before serving.

If hake is not available, cod can be used instead for this appetising dish.

STEAMED FISH WITH WINE
AND TARRAGON SAUCE

(*serves* 2)

2 pieces of white fish, skinned

Sauce
300 ml/½ pint dry white wine
3 sprigs tarragon
50 g/2 oz butter
1 tblsp flour
150 ml/¼ pint fish or chicken stock
50 g/2 oz fromage frais
sea salt and freshly ground black pepper

To steam fish: place the skinned fillets (folded in three) on an oiled plate over a pan of boiling water. Invert another plate on top of the fish and cook over the steam until done. Meanwhile make the sauce:

Reduce the wine by half, by fast boiling in an open pan. Add the chopped leaves of 2 tarragon sprigs and leave over a low heat until the scent of the herbs is quite strong.

Melt the butter and stir in the flour. Cook for 1 minute, then add the stock and seasoning. Bring to the boil, stirring all the time, until the sauce is smooth and thickened. Add the wine and tarragon mixture and fromage frais.

Just before serving, strain the sauce and add the remaining chopped tarragon leaves.

SMOKED HADDOCK WITH PARSLEY SAUCE

(serves 6)

This is the sort of simple and comforting dish that everyone likes best. It is also the kind of thing that, properly made, earns a life-long reputation for being a good cook! It is best with plain boiled potatoes or light, fluffily creamed potatoes. Serve with plain green beans, a tossed green salad, or a lettuce and onion salad (see p. 101).

2.5 kg/3 lb smoked haddock,
soaked for a few hours in cold water
a few onion rings
6 peppercorns
1 small bay leaf
a few lemon slices

Parsley sauce
50 g/2 oz butter
2 level tblsp flour
300 ml/½ pint poaching liquor
300 ml/½ pint low-fat yogurt
6 tblsp chopped parsley and chives
½ tsp sugar
a little white pepper

Rinse and dry the haddock, slip it off its skin with a sharp knife and cut it into bite-sized chunks.

Put the fish into a pan with the onion, peppercorns, bay leaf and lemon. Cover with fresh water and bring to a simmer. Cook very gently for just as long as it takes for the fish to be done. This may be only a minute or two.

Take out the fish, removing any bones that may still be lurking, and put it into a buttered shallow dish. Cover with a piece of damp greaseproof paper and a lid.

Strain the cooking liquor and measure off 300 ml/½ pint for the sauce.

Melt the butter in a pan and stir in the flour. Strain in the fish stock, a little at a time, and cook gently, stirring, to make a smooth sauce.

Whisk in the yogurt and add the chopped herbs and the sugar and pepper. It will probably not need salt but you can taste it to see.

When the sauce is quite hot again, pour it over the waiting fish and serve immediately.

Note: This sauce should be about as thick as pouring cream. If it is any thicker, use the fish liquor to thin the sauce to the right consistency.

NEW POTATOES WITH SMOKED HADDOCK AND CHIVES
(*serves 4*)

700–900 g/1½–2 lb new potatoes
350 g/12 oz smoked haddock (or cod)
1 Spanish onion
1 bay leaf
4 tblsp olive oil
2 tsp coriander seeds, crushed
1 tblsp Dijon mustard
plenty of ground black pepper
1 teacup snipped chives
juice of 1 small lemon

This can be served hot, warm or cold and makes a lovely picnic dish. Wash and boil or steam the new potatoes. Rinse the fish and pat it dry. (Soak it first if you suspect that it is too salty.) Poach it very gently, in water to barely cover, for a few minutes. Drain again, divide it into bite-sized chunks and pick out any bones. Put in a dish, together with the potatoes. Soften the onion in 2 tblsp oil with a bay leaf and crushed coriander seeds.

Add the mustard to this. When the onion is transparent and soft, remove the bay leaf and tip this mixture over the potato and fish dish. Turn all together gently with the addition of the rest of the oil, juice of the lemon, pepper to taste (you may or may not need a little sea salt too) and the snipped fresh chives.

MACKEREL WITH LEMON AND BAY LEAVES

(serves 4)

4 mackerel, cleaned and heads removed
seasoned flour to toss
3 tblsp sunflower or olive oil
2 large Spanish onions, sliced
1 lemon, thinly sliced
2 bay leaves, crumbled
sea salt and freshly ground black pepper

Toss the mackerel in the seasoned flour and fry on each side in the oil, until cooked through. Transfer to heated serving dish and keep warm. Add the onions, lemon slices and bay leaves to the oil in the pan and cook gently until soft. Season to taste. Spoon it over the fish and serve.

Note: Mackerel must always be utterly fresh, with bright eyes and sparkling silver body. Ask your fishmonger to clean the fish and remove the heads.

MACKEREL WITH SOUR CREAM AND CHIVES

(serves 2)

This is one of those simple dishes that is truly excellent. It is a Norwegian recipe, and so is inevitably served with boiled potatoes – very good too!

2 mackerel, filleted and heads removed
1 tblsp flour
sea salt and pepper
1 tblsp sunflower oil
a small carton of sour cream (or low-fat yogurt)
2 tblsp freshly chopped chives

Dust the mackerel with flour and season with salt and pepper. Fry each side in the oil. When they are just cooked, pour the sour cream or yogurt and chives on to them. Warm through gently, shuffling the pan so that the fish does not break or stick.

Garnish with a few lettuce leaves.

GRILLED MACKEREL WITH GOOSEBERRY SAUCE

(serves 4–6)

4–6 mackerel, filleted
450 g/1 lb gooseberries, topped and tailed and rinsed
2 tblsp water or white wine
3 tblsp castor sugar_
1 tsp crushed coriander seeds

Wash and dry mackerel. Place under a medium grill for 10 minutes, turning once. Meanwhile, put the gooseberries in a good saucepan with the water (or wine). Simmer gently until they are soft. Push through a sieve. Return to the rinsed pan and add the sugar and crushed coriander seeds. Stir gently until the sugar has dissolved and the sauce is a beautiful purée about as thick as double cream.

Serve warm with the grilled mackerel.

MACARONI AND TUNA FISH PIE

(serves 10)

Serve this lovely easy pasta dish in a big enamelled roasting tin or gratin dish. The courgettes give it a crunch and the garlicky tomatoes on the top add a little sharpness to the creaminess. Good for a late-night supper – prepare ahead and just reheat.

450 g/1 lb pasta quills (penne) or largish macaroni
3 (200 g/7 oz) tins tuna fish in brine, drained
450 g/1 lb courgettes, in 2.5 cm/1 inch lengths
100 g/¼ lb butter
(sounds a lot but it's for 10 people!)
5 heaped tblsp flour
1.8 litres/3 pints skimmed milk
sea salt and freshly ground pepper
450 g/1 lb tomatoes, skinned and sliced
2–3 tblsp sunflower oil
1 clove garlic crushed
50 g/2 oz Parmesan cheese, grated

Boil the penne or macaroni in plenty of salted water and keep a careful watch over it so that it does not overcook. It should be cooked but still firm and not at all soft or slushy. Drain well and rinse under cold water. Drain again. Turn it into the ovenproof dish.

Break up the chunks of tuna a little with a fork and add them to the pasta. Boil the courgettes until just done but still quite firm and crunchy.

Now make a bechamel (white) sauce. Melt the butter in a good stout saucepan over a gentle heat. Stir in the flour and blend together well. Pour in the milk, a little at a time, and whisk and stir while you bring it to the boil. Keep cooking, whisking and stirring (so that bottom does not 'catch' and brown) until all or most of the milk is used up and you have a lovely sauce as thick as pouring cream.

Season and taste this, remembering that the tuna has added salt.

Strain the sauce over the pasta and tuna. Add the cooked, drained courgettes and mix everything together gently.

Fry the tomatoes and garlic in oil. Lay them evenly over the dish.

Sprinkle the top with Parmesan. Brown in the oven for 10–15 minutes (200°C, Gas Mark 6, 400°F).

Or if it suits you better the dish can be made in advance (say, that morning) and reheated in a more gentle oven (190°C, Gas Mark 5, 375°F) for half an hour or until piping hot.

I serve with this a large tossed salad made up of leafy greens, some red lettuce (radicchio) and thinly sliced cucumber. Black olives pitted and halved add colour; about 20 will be plenty.

FISH PIE

(serves 6)

1 litre/1¾ pints milk
1 small onion, peeled and sliced
1 twist of lemon peel
1 small bay leaf
700 g/1½ lb white fish fillets, such as cod or haddock
225 g/½ lb smoked haddock fillet
3 tblsp sunflower oil
4 tblsp flour
100 g/¼ lb peas, lightly cooked
4 tomatoes, skinned, deseeded and chopped
2 tblsp finely chopped parsley
1 tblsp chopped fresh dill (or 2 tsp dried dill)
sea salt and white pepper
1 kg/2 lb freshly cooked mashed potato

Put the milk, onion, lemon peel and bay leaf into a saucepan and bring to the boil. Set this aside for the flavours to infuse in the milk. Meanwhile slip the fish (both fresh and smoked) off its skin with a sharp knife.

Cut the fish into bite-sized chunks (not too small) and remove any bones. Put the fish into the milk and bring to a simmer. Simmer for one or two minutes only. Take out the fish chunks with a perforated spoon and lay them in a large pie dish. Check again for bones.

Strain the milk into a jug. Wash and dry the saucepan and return it to the cooker with the oil and flour. Mix together over a gentle heat with a wooden spoon. Make a sauce by pouring in some of the strained milk, bring to the boil, stir well with a whisk and repeat until the sauce is like thick cream.

Add the cooked peas, tomatoes and dill to the fish. Add sea salt and pepper sparingly. Pour the sauce over this and mix together gently. Taste for seasoning.

Pile hot mashed potato on the top of the fish and put the dish into a moderately hot oven (190°C, Gas Mark 5, 375°F) for 20–25 minutes. Serve piping hot with a tossed salad.

This dish is popular with all ages. It can be made grander by using some salmon, scallops or shelled prawns, but the nice thing about it is the little bit of colour from the peas and tomatoes, and the extra flavour from smoked fish.

TROUT WITH ALMONDS

(serves 6)

A popular way of cooking trout in England and Scandinavia, where the lovely fresh fish is in need of no further adornment.

6 trout
seasoned flour to toss
olive oil
100 g/4 oz flaked almonds
sea salt
lemon wedges

Clean the fish and remove the heads, or ask the fishmonger to do it for you. Toss the trout in seasoned flour. Heat just sufficient oil in a heavy-bottomed frying pan and add the fish. Cook for 3–4 minutes on each side, shuffling the pan to make sure the fish does not stick.

Meanwhile, gently fry the almonds in 1 tblsp oil until golden on both sides. Drain on kitchen paper and sprinkle with salt.

Serve the trout scattered with the almonds and surrounded by lemon wedges.

TROUT A LA MEUNIÈRE

(serves 4)

So called because it is dusty with flour like the miller's wife.

4 trout
olive oil
flour for dredging
sea salt and pepper
2 lemons
parsley, washed and dried

Ask your fishmonger to clean the trout and remove the heads.

Wash the fish and pat dry. Rub them with a little oil and dust on each side with flour, shaking off any excess. Season lightly.

Heat the oil in a good frying pan that will take all four fish. Put in the trout and fry gently, shuffling the pan so that the fish doesn't stick, until they are barely cooked on one side. Turn them over carefully and cook the other side (which will cook quicker).

Slip the trout on to a hot serving dish and keep warm. Now remove the frying pan from the heat and pour in the juice of 1 lemon. Add 2 tblsp chopped parsley, stir and then pour quickly over the trout.

Garnish with the other lemon cut into wedges and some sprigs of parsley in a bunch.

Serve this with steamed potatoes. (A metal steamer goes into the saucepan and can be bought in good supermarkets for under £2.)

A lettuce and onion salad would be lovely with the trout. Make it like this:

> 1 or 2 heads of lettuce (depending on their size)
> 1 small onion, peeled and sliced wafer thin
> 3 tblsp olive oil
> 1 tblsp wine vinegar
> 1 tsp sugar
> a little sea salt and pepper

Wash and dry the lettuce and tear it up gently into an attractive bowl. Separate and scatter some of the onion rings. Sprinkle the oil on the onion and lettuce and turn them carefully until they have a shiny coating. Drizzle the vinegar, sugar, salt and pepper over. Give the salad another turn.

FILLET OF TURBOT WITH STUFFED BRAISED LETTUCE LEAVES

(serves 4)

Braised lettuce
4 good-sized lettuce leaves
175 g/6 oz mushrooms, very finely chopped
grated rind of ½ lemon
25 g/1 oz butter
a little sea salt and pepper

4 fillets of turbot, skin removed
4 tblsp white wine
1 tblsp lemon juice
sea salt and pepper
4 tblsp fromage frais

Blanch the lettuce leaves for only a second in boiling water. Cool in a bowl of cold water, drain well and pat dry with kitchen paper. Cook the mushrooms lightly with lemon rind in butter. Season, stuff the lettuce leaves with the mixture when it is cool, forming them into neat bright green parcels.

Put the fish fillets in a shallow ovenproof dish with the white wine, lemon juice, seasoning and a little water. Cover and put in a moderate oven (190°C, Gas Mark 5, 375°F) for 15–20 minutes, or until the fish is *just* cooked.

The stuffed lettuce leaves should warm through gently in a covered dish on the shelf below. Keep the fillets warm while you boil up the juices in a pan to reduce them to about 4 tablespoons. Finish by whisking in the fromage frais.

Place a piece of fish on each plate, and a stuffed lettuce leaf. Serve with the sauce spooned over the fish.

TO BAKE A PIECE OF SALMON

Here is a simple fail-safe method for baking salmon in foil.

175 g/6 oz per serving is about right. Preheat the oven to 180°C, Gas Mark 4, 350°F. Oil the salmon well and sprinkle with a few drops of lemon juice and a little sea salt and pepper. Wrap loosely in oiled foil. Bake for 20 minutes per 450 g/pound and 10 minutes over.

Trout can be baked in the same way.

The trout should be cleaned (ask your fishmonger if you are not sure how).

Take whole trout of about 275 g/10 oz to 350 g/12 oz for each person. If you have lemon balm growing in the window-box or garden, pick a few sprigs, rinse them and lay them in the cavity of the trout. Wrap each fish in oiled foil, with a little sea salt and pepper as above.

Bake for 20–25 minutes at 180°C, Gas Mark 4, 350°F.

BAKED SALMON WITH FRESH GINGER
AND SPRING ONIONS

(serves 4)

550 g/1¼ lb middle cut of salmon
2.5 cm/1 inch fresh, peeled ginger
8 spring onions
soy sauce
sunflower oil
¼ lemon

Clean the salmon thoroughly, taking care to wash away the blood in a vein down the backbone.

Cut the ginger into little matchsticks. Chop the white part of the spring onions and mix them with the ginger and a tablespoon of soy sauce.

Rub the salmon with oil and put the ginger, spring onion and soy sauce inside the fish. Wrap carefully in foil.

Bake for 30 minutes in the oven at 180°C, Gas Mark 4, 350°F. Be careful not to overcook the fish; it should just come away from the bone.

Serve with a squeeze of lemon and soy sauce.

SALMON FISHCAKES

(serves 6)

700 g/1½ lb cooked salmon
700 g/1½ lb potatoes
2 tblsp chopped dill
2 tblsp chopped olives
sea salt and pepper
1 egg and a little milk
breadcrumbs
dill and lemon for garnish

If you have the tail end of a cooked salmon left over it will do perfectly for these. Here grated potatoes are used instead of the more usual mashed potato. It seems to make the fishcakes lighter.

Skin and bone the salmon carefully and separate it into flakes with a fork. Peel the potatoes and cook them for 18 minutes – they should be cooked but still firm. Grate the potatoes when they are cold and mix them with the salmon. Add the chopped herbs and season with sea salt and pepper.

Form the mixture into fishcakes. Lightly mix the egg and milk in a shallow bowl. Dip the fishcakes in the egg and milk and then coat them in breadcrumbs (not the orange packet sort). A good way to do this is to put the crumbs in a non-stick saucepan and put the salmon cakes in one at a time, moving them about gently until they are well coated.

Grill gently until the outside is golden and the inside is well warmed through. Serve with a sprig of dill and a wedge of lemon.

SALT FISH CHOWDER

(serves 6)

This substantial fish soup is good for a picnic on a cold day. Carry in a big, wide-mouthed Thermos. Follow with a salad and fresh fruit with fruit cake.

1 kg/2 lb fish bones, including a salmon head if possible
3 tblsp olive oil
1 onion, finely chopped
2 cloves garlic, crushed
1.5 cm/½ inch cube of ginger, peeled and grated
1 small sweet red pepper
2 small chilli peppers, deseeded
2 leeks, chopped
1 tin of Italian peeled, chopped tomatoes
6 medium potatoes, peeled and diced
a little chopped thyme, lemon thyme or fennel
1 tsp sugar
225 g/8 oz salt cod or haddock, rinsed and cut into squares
grated rind of 1 lemon
black pepper
150 ml/¼ pint mayonnaise (see p. 192)
6 rounds of French bread

Simmer the bones and trimmings for about 40 minutes in enough water to barely cover. (I use a pressure cooker for this as it takes only 15 minutes.) Strain. Wrap the bones in newspaper and discard.

Put the olive oil in a large, thick-bottomed saucepan and gently soften the onion, garlic, ginger, red pepper, chillies, leeks, tomatoes, potatoes and herbs. After turning these carefully in the oil for 5–10 minutes, add the strained fish stock. Simmer all together for 25 minutes and then slip in the fish. Poach for a few minutes more until the fish is cooked. Now taste for seasoning and add the lemon rind and pepper. Taste again.

Serve in bowls with a round of French bread spread with a spoonful of garlic mayonnaise lowered into each.

SEAFOOD PANCAKES
(serves 8–10)
Basic pancake batter (see p. 75)

Make thin pancakes with batter that has stood for at least half an hour.

Filling
225 g/8 oz fillet of plaice
100 g/4 oz monkfish, trimmed of skin and bone
6 scallops
water to barely cover, with lemon juice and seasoning

Sauce
2 tblsp sunflower oil
2 tblsp flour
300 ml/½ pint milk
100 g/4 oz tomatoes, skinned, deseeded and diced
1 tsp tomatoe purée
2 tblsp brandy
4 tblsp low-fat yogurt
sea salt and white pepper
grated Parmesan to sprinkle on top

Skin the plaice and cut it into slices. Rinse and slice the scallops into three, reserving the coral.

Put the fish pieces and the scallop slices and corals into a small pan with the acidulated water. Bring to a simmer and cook for a minute or two until the fish pieces are barely done. Now strain off the fish liquor and boil it down until there is only a couple of tablespoonfuls left.

Make a sauce by warming the oil in a saucepan and stirring in the flour. Gradually work in the milk, stirring and bringing it to the boil at each addition of milk. Add the tomatoes and then the tomato purée, brandy, yogurt and seasoning, tasting carefully for flavour. Thin the sauce with the fish liquor. It should be about as thick as pouring cream.

Fold one-third of the sauce into the fish. Put a good table-spoon of the mixture on to each pancake, fold over and lay alongside each other in a greased, heatproof dish.

Pour the rest of the sauce on top and sprinkle with Parmesan. Warm through carefully. Sprinkle with Parmesan again and flash under a hot grill until the top is golden.

Seven

POULTRY AND GAME

Chicken, the white meat of turkey and all game closely follow fish as the best source of protein for a healthy heart. Chicken and turkey can be prepared in such a wide variety of ways. They are low in harmful fats, especially when the skin is removed. Compared with domestically reared creatures, all game is low in fat. I suppose that the struggle of surviving in the wild keeps them lean!

GRILLED CHICKEN

A grilled chicken is one of the nicest foods at any time, and particularly in summer. Everybody likes it and chickens are reasonably priced, within even the most slender means.

For good grilled chicken buy a first-rate fresh bird – or chicken quarters if you can't face jointing the bird yourself, but remember that chicken pieces are more expensive.

Rub the pieces with lemon juice, fresh lemon thyme or marjoram, sea salt and pepper. Sprinkle with olive oil.

Heat the grill. Place the chicken on the wire grid, skin side up. Turn after 5 minutes and seal the other side. Turn them over again and baste with juices from the pan. Lower the heat a little and cook for another 5 minutes on each side (a total grilling time of about 20 minutes).

The chicken joints should be golden brown with slightly crispy skin. They must be cooked so that the juices run clear, not pink, at the deepest part of the joint when gently pierced with a skewer.

Spread a mixture of salad leaves and roughly chopped herbs (parsley, chives, a little mint, a little fennel) on a long dish. Put the chicken on to this bed of green and add a few generous lemon wedges.

Drain off the fat then sprinkle the hot juices over all before serving, together with some more pepper, if you like, and a few drops of fresh lemon juice.

ROAST CHICKEN WITH HERBS

(serves 4)

1 1.5 kg/3–3½lb roasting chicken, with giblets
25 g/1 oz butter
sea salt and freshly ground black pepper
chopped tarragon or thyme
twist of lemon peel
1 clove garlic, crushed
300 ml/½ pint hot water
cornflour to thicken
white wine or lemon juice (see method)

Remove the giblets from the chicken. Sprinkle a small knob of the butter with salt, pepper and tarragon and pop it inside the chicken with the twist of lemon peel and the crushed clove of garlic. Rub the chicken with the remaining butter and scatter tarragon over it. Season the bird lightly. Place in a roasting tin with the giblets, and pour in the hot water. Cover the tin loosely with foil, and cook in a moderately hot oven (200°C, Gas Mark 6, 400°F) for about 1¼ hours. Check occasionally during cooking that the liquid in the tin has not dried out – add a little more water if it looks low.

When the chicken is ready the leg joints should move freely, and when pierced with a fine skewer the juice that runs should be clear, not pink. Lift the bird on to a hot carving dish, remove the giblets and turn your attention to the beautiful juices left in the pan. Drain off the fat then thicken them with a little cornflour moistened in cold water. Add a dash of white wine, or a squeeze of lemon juice, according to taste. Strain and serve.

CHICKEN IN WHITE WINE
(serves 4)

2 tblsp sunflower oil
2 medium onions, peeled and thinly sliced
1 1.5 kg/3–3½ lb chicken, jointed
225 g/8 oz button mushrooms, wiped and sliced
2 tblsp flour
2 tsp freshly chopped tarragon leaves
4 tomatoes, peeled and chopped
350 ml/12 fl oz (½ bottle) dry white wine
100 g/4 oz fromage frais

Heat the oil in a flameproof casserole and cook the onion until soft and golden. Add the chicken pieces and turn occasionally for about 10 minutes over a gentle heat. Add the button mushrooms (cap ones discolour the dish) and sprinkle the flour on top. Stir everything together gently. Add the tarragon. Pour in the white wine by degrees, bring to the boil, reduce the heat and simmer, covered, for about 20 minutes. Add the fromage frais towards the end of the cooking time and leave uncovered if the sauce needs to be reduced a little.

ROAST CHICKEN WITH FROMAGE FRAIS AND LEMON
(serves 4)

1.5 kg/3–3½ lb roasting chicken with giblets
175 g/6 oz fromage frais
1 lemon
sea salt and pepper
a little sunflower oil
450 ml/¾ pint hot water
0.75 kg/1½–2 lb small new potatoes, washed

Remove the giblets from the bird and lay them in a large roasting tin.

Grate the rind of the lemon into the fromage frais and add a little salt and pepper. Stuff the cavity of the bird with this.

Rub the skin of the chicken with a little oil. Place in the roasting tin on the giblets.

Pour in 450 ml/¾ pint of water with the juice of the lemon. Now put the little potatoes all around the chicken in the tin.

Cover loosely with a piece of foil (just the chicken; leave the rest of the tin uncovered).

Cook in a moderately hot oven (200°C, Gas Mark 6, 400°F) for 1½ hours.

The chicken is ready when the leg joints move freely, and when pierced with a fine skewer the juice that runs should be clear, not pink. Test the potatoes too.

Lift the chicken on to a warm dish to carve. Surround with the little potatoes. Remove the giblets and reserve them for making soup.

NORMANDY CHICKEN

(serves 4)

1 1.5 kg/3–3½ lb chicken
2 cooking apples
3 outer sticks celery
1 large onion, peeled and sliced
1 tsp tarragon
1 tblsp flour
a little sunflower oil
300 ml/½ pint dry white wine or cider
300 ml/½ pint chicken giblet stock
sea salt and freshly ground pepper
150 ml/¼ pint fromage frais

Garnish
4 dessert apples, peeled
2 tblsp sunflower oil
2 tblsp castor sugar
sprigs of watercress

Heat a little oil in a flameproof casserole and brown the chicken carefully all over. Peel, core and cut up the cooking apples and clean and chop the celery. Take out the chicken and set aside. Add the onion, apples, tarragon and celery to the casserole and cook for 5 minutes. Shake the flour over the mixture and gently stir in the wine or cider and the stock. Season. Return the chicken to the casserole and put on the lid. Simmer gently on top of the stove for 35–40 minutes, or until the chicken is cooked through.

Meanwhile, core the dessert apples and cut into rings. Fry them lightly in oil and dust with castor sugar.

Carve the chicken on to a heated serving dish. Add the fromage frais to the vegetables in the casserole and heat through. Tip the vegetables and sauce into a sieve, and mash the apples and vegetables through as much as possible. Return to the casserole, reheat and pour over and around the chicken.

Cook the remainder of the head of celery to serve with the chicken. Garnish the chicken with fried apple rings and sprigs of watercress.

CHICKEN WITH VINEGAR SAUCE

(serves 4)

This sauce is not sharp as you might imagine from the title, but has a subtle flavour.

1 chicken, weighing 1.4 kg/3 lb, jointed
sea salt and pepper
2 tblsp flour
1 tblsp sunflower oil

Sauce
4 tblsp white wine vinegar
1 onion, finely chopped
1 glass of white wine
1 tsp tomato purée
½ tblsp Dijon mustard
300 ml/½ pint chicken stock

Garnish
2 peeled, deseeded and chopped tomatoes
parsley

Coat the chicken pieces in flour and season with salt and pepper. Fry them until golden in the oil.

Take the chicken pieces out and put all the ingredients for the sauce into the pan that the chicken has been cooking in. Stir around the sides to bring in any of the juices. Boil to reduce it in volume until there is enough liquid to almost cover the chicken. Replace the chicken pieces in the sauce. Cover the pan and reduce the heat. Simmer for about 15 minutes – or just as long as it takes to finish cooking the joints right through. It is, however, really important not to *overcook* the chicken, so keep an eye on this!

To serve, put the chicken on a hot serving dish, reduce the sauce if there is too much and then strain it over the chicken. Put the tomato pieces on the top and decorate the dish with parsley.

Serve simply with potatoes or rice and a green salad.

CHICKEN EN COCOTTE

(serves 4)

Serve this with noodles, rice or boiled potatoes.

1 1.5 kg/3–3½ lb chicken, jointed
sea salt and freshly ground black pepper
2 tblsp olive oil
50 g/2 oz lean smoked ham, diced
4 small onions, chopped
1 clove garlic, crushed
2 tblsp brandy
6 tomatoes, peeled and chopped
3 carrots, chopped
2 sticks celery, cut into 4 cm/1½ inch lengths
¼ tsp chopped thyme
1 bay leaf
300 ml/½ pint red wine
12 pitted black olives
chopped parsley to garnish

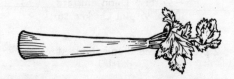

Season the chicken portions with salt and pepper. Heat the oil in a casserole or sauté pan and add the diced ham and chicken pieces. Cook, turning, until golden. Take out the meats and set aside.

Fry the onions and garlic in the pan, stirring, until softened. Return the chicken and ham to the pan. Pour on the brandy and flambé the meats. Now add the tomatoes, carrots, celery, thyme, bay leaf and red wine. Bring to the boil, add the olives, cover and simmer for about 30 minutes, until the chicken and vegetables are tender. Remove the bay leaf before serving and sprinkle with chopped parsley.

PAPRIKA CHICKEN

(serves 4)

1 1.5 kg/3–3½ lb chicken
2 tblsp sunflower oil
1 tsp caraway seeds
grated rind of ½ orange
300 ml/½ pint giblet stock

Sauce
1 tblsp sunflower oil
1 onion, finely chopped
1 clove garlic, crushed
2 tblsp paprika
1 tblsp flour
225 g/8 oz tomatoes, peeled and chopped
150 ml/¼ pint white wine or cider
2 caps tinned pimiento, chopped
sea salt and freshly ground black pepper
150 ml/¼ pint natural low-fat yogurt

Brush the chicken with the oil and sprinkle the caraway and orange rind inside and out. Stand it in a roasting tin, pour the giblet stock around, cover loosely with greaseproof paper or foil and cook in a moderately hot oven (200°C, Gas Mark 6, 400°F) for 1¼ hours.

Meanwhile, prepare the sauce. Heat the oil and cook the onion and garlic until quite soft. Sprinkle the paprika and flour on to the onion and mix in well. Add the tomatoes, white wine or cider, chopped pimiento and seasoning. Bring to the boil, stirring constantly, and simmer until well reduced. Just before serving, remove from the heat and stir in the yogurt.

Joint or carve the cooked chicken on to a hot dish and pour the sauce over it. Serve with noodles tossed in a little butter and sprinkled with chopped parsley.

CHICKEN PIE

(serves 4)

350 g/12 oz shortcrust pastry (see p. 205)
2 young carrots, sliced
1 113 g/4 oz packet frozen mixed peas and sweetcorn
25 g/1 oz butter
1 tblsp flour
300 ml/½ pint skimmed milk
225 g/8 oz cooked chicken, chopped
grated rind of 1 lemon
2 tblsp chopped parsley
sea salt and black pepper
parsley sprig to garnish

First make the pastry. Cover and chill in the refrigerator while making the filling. Cook the carrots, peas and sweetcorn, drain and set aside. Melt the butter and stir the flour into it. Add the milk, half at a time, and stir over a low heat until it has been simmering for several minutes. Combine the carrots, peas, sweetcorn, chicken, lemon rind and parsley all together. Mix into the sauce and season to taste.

Line the base of a greased and floured baking tin with half the pastry rolled out thinly. Prick with a fork and dampen the edges. Fill with chicken mixture, roll out the remaining pastry and lay on top, pressing down the edges to seal. Trim the edges and knock up, brush with skimmed milk and bake in a moderately hot oven (190°C, Gas Mark 5, 375°F) for about 40 minutes. Garnish with a parsley sprig.

CHICKEN WITH MUSTARD AND TARRAGON

(serves 6)

1 1.5–1.75 kg/3½–4 lb chicken, with giblets
1 tblsp sunflower oil
sea salt and freshly ground black pepper
twist of lemon peel
sprig of tarragon
300 ml/½ pint water
25 g/1 oz butter
1 tblsp flour
150 ml/¼ pint dry white wine
3 tsp Dijon mustard
2 tblsp chopped tarragon
75 g/3 oz Gruyère cheese, grated

Brush the bird all over with oil and sprinkle with salt and pepper. Tuck the twist of lemon peel and sprig of tarragon inside the chicken. Place over the giblets in a roasting tin, pour in the water and cover the tin loosely with foil or greaseproof paper. Cook in a moderately hot oven (200°C, Gas Mark 6, 400°F) for 1¼–1½ hours, until cooked. Take up the chicken and joint and carve it. Lay the pieces on a hot dish and cover with the foil or greaseproof paper. Keep warm while you make the sauce.

Melt the butter in a saucepan. Stir the flour into it and cook for 1 minute. Having drained off the fat and strained the juices from the roasting tin, stir the juices in and then add the white wine. Bring to the boil, stirring constantly, and flavour with the mustard and tarragon. Stir into it the grated cheese. Simmer, stirring, for a few minutes. Pour the sauce over the chicken and serve immediately.

STUFFED POT-ROASTED CHICKEN

(serves 6)

75 g/3 oz long-grain rice
1 1.75 kg/4 lb chicken, with giblets
50 g/2 oz sultanas
1 small red sweet pepper, deseeded and chopped
grated rind of 1 lemon
sea salt and freshly ground black pepper
0.5 kg/1 lb onions, quartered
0.5 kg/1 lb baby carrots
0.5 kg/1 lb small potatoes, peeled and halved
¼ tsp chopped rosemary
300 ml/½ pint dry cider
little lemon juice
little sunflower oil

Cook the rice in boiling salted water for 10 minutes, until just tender. Drain well. Mix together the cooked rice, sultanas, red pepper, grated lemon rind and seasoning. Stuff the chicken with this mixture.

Grease a casserole dish large enough to take the chicken comfortably. Place the onions, carrots and tomatoes in the bottom, brush the chicken with the oil, sprinkle with the rosemary and lay it on top. Pour the cider around the chicken.

Cover the casserole and cook in a moderate oven (180°C, Gas Mark 4, 350°F) for 2 hours, until the chicken is tender. Remove the lid for the last 10 minutes to brown the bird.

Lift out the chicken and place on a hot serving dish. Remove the vegetables carefully with a slotted spoon and arrange around the bird. Strain the juices from the casserole into a small pan, skim and add a squeeze of lemon juice. Reheat and serve separately in a jug or sauce boat.

For accompaniment, this needs only plain boiled potatoes tossed in some finely chopped parsley. Follow with a crisp green salad. It's really delicious!

COLD LEMON CHICKEN

(serves 6)

1 1.5–2 kg/3½–4 lb chicken
1 onion, peeled and sliced
225 g/8 oz carrots, peeled and cut into little strips
juice of 1 lemon
sea salt and pepper
2 egg yolks
1 tblsp cornflour
300 ml/½ pint low-fat yogurt
parsley or mint for garnish
lemon wedges

Place the chicken in a saucepan with the giblets, onion and carrot. Cover with water, add 2 twists of lemon peel and seasoning, then cover the pan and simmer for about 45–55 minutes, until tender. Cool the chicken and remove the flesh from the bones. Cut the meat into bite-sized pieces and discard the skin.

Blend together about 300 ml/½ pint of the skimmed, strained stock with the lemon juice, the egg yolks and cornflour. Cook this carefully in a double boiler until the sauce is smooth and coats the back of a wooden spoon. Cool and beat in the yogurt. Thin with a little more chicken stock if necessary and adjust the seasoning.

Lay the chicken on a serving dish and mask with the lemon sauce.

Garnish with parsley or mint and more lemon, cut in wedges.

Accompany with a tossed green salad and perhaps a tomato salad. A dish of sliced avocado pear and kiwi fruit goes well with it too.

COCK-A-LEEKIE

(serves 4–6)

1 large boiling fowl
6 leeks
50g/2oz pearl barley, previously soaked and drained
1 tsp sea salt
10 black peppercorns
chopped parsley

Put the bird on a trivet in a saucepan and surround with washed, thickly cut leeks and the pearl barley (also washed). Cover with cold water, bring to the boil and allow to simmer very gently – it should just shiver, not boil. Cook like this for about 2 hours, adding more boiling water if necessary. To serve, cut the chicken in small pieces free from skin and bone. Allow liquid to cool and then skim off the fat. All this can be done in advance. Reheat (gently – no boiling!). Serve in soup plates with chicken, leeks, barley and stock. Sprinkle with parsley. Good with plain boiled potatoes or hunks of bread.

TURKEY IN PERNOD

(serves 6)

1 3–3.5kg/6–7lb turkey
2 tblsp sunflower oil
1 tblsp chopped thyme
1 small onion, chopped
2 sticks celery, chopped
4 medium carrots, chopped
4 tblsp Pernod
1 cup water

Stuffing
75g/3oz fresh white breadcrumbs
50g/2oz butter, melted
grated rind of 1½ lemons
4 tblsp chopped parsley
½ tsp chopped thyme
sea salt and freshly ground black pepper
100g/4oz green grapes, halved and pipped

Mix together the stuffing ingredients and spoon into the bird. Brush the turkey all over with oil and sprinkle with the chopped thyme. Lay the onion, celery and carrots in the base of a large oblong casserole dish or roasting tin. Place the turkey on the bed of vegetables and pour the Pernod and water around it. Cover and cook in a moderately hot oven (190°C, Gas Mark 5, 375°F) for about 2½–3 hours. Baste from time to time with the pan juices. Add a little hot giblet stock or water, if necessary, to keep the dish moist.

The turkey will be succulent and tender. Slice the flesh, and serve with a spoonful of stuffing and the strained juices from the casserole.

BAKED DEVILLED CHICKEN

(serves 4)

8 chicken thighs
(remove the skin first to reduce the fat)
2 tblsp mango chutney
2 tsp Dijon mustard
1 clove garlic, crushed
¼ tsp cayenne pepper
1 tblsp Worcestershire sauce
1 tblsp tamari
2 tblsp tomato ketchup

Lay the chicken joints quite close to each other in a greased shallow ovenproof dish.

Mix together in a bowl the chutney, mustard, crushed garlic, cayenne, Worcestershire sauce, tamari and ketchup. Pour this over the chicken.

Put into a pre-heated oven (180°C, Gas Mark 4, 350°F) for 1–1½ hours. If the chicken juices still run pink when pierced, cook a little longer until they run clear.

Good with a rice salad that has a sliced banana mixed in at the last minute.

GRILLED DEVILLED CHICKEN

(serves 4)

1 1.5 kg/3–3½ lb chicken, jointed and skinned,
or 4 chicken portions, skinned
1 tblsp French mustard
1 tsp grated ginger
½ tsp sea salt
1 tsp freshly ground black pepper
2 tsp honey
juice of 1 lemon
2 tblsp sunflower oil

Place the chicken portions in a shallow ovenproof dish. Mix together the mustard, fresh ginger, salt, pepper, honey and lemon juice. Use to coat the chicken portions and leave them to marinate for several hours, turning occasionally.

Sprinkle the oil over the chicken portions and place under a preheated grill, not too close. Allow 10–15 minutes on each side. This is especially good when cooked on an outside barbecue or fire.

Serve with a green salad and rice pilaf (see p. 79).

A SPANISH PAELLA

(serves 6)

1 1.5 kg/3–3½ lb chicken, with giblets
1 tblsp olive oil
sea salt and pepper
175 g/6 oz frozen peas, cooked and drained
1 tin sweetcorn, drained
1 large Spanish onion
2 cloves garlic
1 good-sized sweet red pepper
225 g/8 oz ripe, red tomatoes, peeled and deseeded
100 g/4 oz Spanish sausage (chorizo), skinned and sliced

Garnish
12 cooked prawns in their shells
chopped parsley
black olives
lemon wedges

Stand the chicken on its giblets in a roasting tin. Oil the skin of the bird all over and season it lightly with salt and pepper.

Pour half a pint of water into the tin and place a piece of foil loosely over the chicken. Roast in a preheated oven (200°C, Gas Mark 6, 400°F) for 1½ hours; this way the chicken part roasts and part steams and will remain very moist and tender. When it is cooked, set aside to cool so that the juices are set and it is easier to handle.

Boil the rice in plenty of fast-boiling water until it is just cooked, but by no means overcooked. This will take about 9 minutes. Test a few grains by cooling them in a little cold water. Drain and refresh the rice with a little cold water.

Add the peas and sweetcorn to the rice.

Peel and chop the onion. Crush the garlic to a paste with sea salt. Sauté them gently in olive oil. Meanwhile prepare the pepper, discarding the pith and pips and chopping it roughly, and add to the onion and continue to cook gently. Add the chopped tomatoes and stir and cook until everything is soft.

Fry the chorizo sausage quickly and drain it on kitchen paper (throw away the fat left in the pan). Add the sausage to the onion and rice.

Strip the flesh off the chicken and discard the skin. Tear the flesh into bite-sized pieces and put the bones and carcass aside for making stock. Skim the fat off the top of the chicken juices in the roasting pan.

Fold the chicken pieces into the rice mixture, and also add the skimmed cooking juices.

Before serving, heat everything through thoroughly and adjust seasoning.

Pile the paella on to a large hot serving dish and surround it with the prawns and olives. Dredge a good handful of chopped parsley down the centre. The colours are lovely.

Optional: The paella in Spain varies from region to region and from one kitchen to another. It often includes shellfish – such as mussels and prawns – and is usually seasoned with a saffron-coloured spice which comes in packets. Shellfish is high in cholesterol, so I have avoided it in this recipe, except for the garnish of prawns which can be left by anyone following a strict regime.

DUCK

Duck is a delicious but uneconomical bird and for a healthy heart it should be an infrequent treat. Weight for weight there is less meat, more fat and bone on a duck than on a chicken. Avoid flat-breasted birds as the breast is the main source of meat.

The stuffing for a duck should be low in fat and quite sharp in flavour. Sage and onion are usual but stuffings with apple are good too. Sometimes I just fill the cavity with some peas – or an apple or a small onion, stuck with a clove.

Prick the bird all over to make the fat run away into the tin. Set the duck on a grid or on its giblets with a little chopped onion and carrot. Roast it in a very hot oven (240°C, Gas Mark 9, 475°F) for 20 minutes, then reduce to moderate setting (190°C, Gas Mark 5, 375°F) for the remainder of the cooking time. It will take longer than the chicken, at least an hour and a half. The juices, when the bird is pricked, should run clear, not pink. Put the duck on a hot dish and keep it warm. Carefully tip away the fat.

Pour orange juice or cider into the tin and scrape around with a wooden spoon to dislodge the pieces which make the gravy. Boil this for a couple of minutes and strain it into a hot gravy boat.

ROAST DUCK WITH SEVILLE ORANGE SAUCE AND STUFFING

(serves 4)

1 2 kg/4½ lb young duck, with giblets
grated rind and juice of 2 Seville oranges
1 tblsp brown sugar (or to taste)
2 tsp cornflour
1 glass white wine (optional)
sea salt

Stuffing
3 tblsp olive oil
100 g/4 oz white breadcrumbs
2 sticks celery
grated rind and juice of 1 Seville orange
sea salt and pepper
1 tblsp sugar
1 tsp powdered cinnamon

Make the stuffing by frying the fresh white breadcrumbs (prepare these in your food processor if you are fortunate enough to have one) in oil with celery and orange rind. Season and stir in the sugar and cinnamon. Sprinkle with the strained orange juice.

Remove the giblets from the duck and put them into a roasting pan. Prick the skin of the duck with a fork (to encourage the fat below the surface to run out during cooking). Put the stuffing in the cavity. Sprinkle the bird with salt and place it on the giblets in the tin. Put into hot oven (220°C, Gas Mark 7, 425°F) for half an hour.

Take the duck out and turn the oven down to a moderate heat (190°C, Gas Mark 5, 375°F). Strew the duck with the grated orange rind and return to the oven for another hour, or until the juices run clear.

Take out the bird carefully and put it in a warm place on a hot serving dish. Carefully tip away the fat from the roasting tin into a bowl. Now stir the orange juice and sugar into the remaining juices in the tin and, with a wooden spoon, mash and work the duck liver into the juices to flavour the gravy.

Slake the cornflour with a little wine (or water) and add the remaining wine (or water) and stir over a gentle heat to cook for a few minutes. Strain into a hot gravy boat or jug. I always serve the gravy under the carved duck (not over it) so as to keep the skin crispy.

Serve a spoonful or two of stuffing on each plate. A salad of watercress and orange, tossed in a little French dressing with the addition of a pinch of curry powder and a couple of spoonfuls of yogurt, is an ideal accompaniment. A purée of potatoes (mashed potatoes) and a dish of braised celery goes beautifully too.

DUCKLING WITH TURNIPS

(serves 4–6)

1 2 kg/4½ lb young duck, with giblets
sea salt
2 carrots, diced
2 sticks celery, finely chopped
bouquet garni
300 ml/½ pint cider
900 g/2 lb turnips, peeled and boiled for 5 minutes

Remove the giblets from the duck and reserve. Prick the duck with a sharp fork, particularly in the fatty areas at the top of the legs. Sprinkle with salt, place on a rack in a roasting tin and cook in a hot oven (220°C, Gas Mark 7, 425°F) for 30 minutes. Take out the duck, remove the rack and pour away all the fat. Return the duck to the roasting tin, sitting it on top of the giblets, carrots, celery, bouquet garni and cider, and with turnips all around. Place a piece of foil loosely over the duck and return the roasting tin to a moderately hot oven (190°C, Gas Mark 5, 375°F) for 1 hour, or until the duck is cooked through and tender. Remove the foil and roast for another 15 minutes to crisp the skin.

Place the duck on a hot serving dish. Surround with the turnips and keep warm. Pour away any fat from the roasting tin and carefully strain the juices remaining in the tin through a sieve. Heat through the sauce and serve separately. Serve with an orange and watercress salad.

DUCK WITH OLIVES

(serves 4)

Roast duck in a tomato and olive sauce, with a little of the cooking juices from the duck.

1 1.5 kg/4 lb duck
450 g/1 lb green olives, stoned
1 litre/1¾ pints clear poultry stock, unsalted
1 cup (300 ml/½ pint) spicy tomato sauce, with very little salt

Cook the olives in a saucepan in three-quarters of the stock and allow to simmer very gently for about 1 hour. Add the tomato sauce and simmer for a further 20 minutes.

Prick the duck's skin to let the fat run out in the cooking. While the sauce is cooking, roast the duck on a rack in a roasting tin in a hot oven at 180°C, Gas Mark 4, 350°F, for about 2 hours. When it is cooked, put it on a warm dish. Tip away the fat carefully from the roasting tin and add some of the stock. Cook to reduce it for a well-flavoured sauce.

Slice the breast and cut off the legs and wings. Arrange on a well-heated serving dish and keep warm. Add the juices from the carved duck to those in the roasting pan and strain them. Bring to the boil. Cover the duck with about a third of the sauce and the olives, and serve the remainder in a sauce boat.

Note: If you prefer crispy skin on the duck, pour the sauce around the carved duck rather than over it.

CASSEROLE OF HARE

(serves 8)

The little bit of chocolate in this recipe sounds odd, but it helps to darken and enrich the dish.

1 hare, jointed
2 tblsp olive oil
100 g/4 oz smoked bacon, trimmed of fat and diced
12 button onions
2 tblsp flour
24 chestnuts, peeled
2 tsp redcurrant jelly
3 small squares dark chocolate, grated

Marinade
1 onion, chopped
1 carrot, chopped
1 tblsp crushed coriander seeds
4 tblsp sunflower or olive oil
¾–1 bottle red wine
sea salt and freshly ground black pepper
bouquet garni
2 cloves garlic, crushed
1 bay leaf

The hare should be adequately hung and carefully jointed by your butcher. It will need to be marinated for a day or two, so plan well ahead.

To prepare the marinade, cook the onion and carrot for a few minutes in the oil, then add the remaining ingredients and simmer for about 15 minutes. Leave to cool, then pour this over the hare portions in a deep casserole. Cover, and turn the meat occasionally. Marinate for 1–2 days.

When you are ready to cook the dish, remove the hare portions and lay on a plate. Keep the marinade in a bowl by the cooker. Rinse and dry the casserole.

Heat the oil in the casserole and brown the bacon and button onions. Take out the onions and reserve. Sprinkle the flour over the bacon and stir. Put in the hare portions, pour in the marinade, stirring to incorporate, and bring gently to the boil. Barely simmer, covered, for 1½–2 hours. Half an hour before the end of the cooking time, add the button onions, chestnuts, redcurrant jelly and grated chocolate.

Remove the hare portions, the button onions and the chestnuts and place on a large hot serving dish. Reduce the sauce if necessary (boil rapidly, stirring, without a lid) and then strain over the meat. Dust with chopped parsley.

Hand redcurrant jelly separately and serve with puréed potatoes and a fresh green vegetable.

RABBIT WITH ROSEMARY AND CALVADOS

(serves 6)

This is an elegant and unusual dish.

1 wild rabbit, jointed
3 tblsp olive oil
2 tblsp flour
1 large onion, peeled and chopped
1 tblsp freshly chopped rosemary
2 tblsp calvados
2 tblsp Dijon mustard
300 ml/½ pint cider
sea salt and freshly ground pepper

The rabbit, preferably wild because it will have more taste, should be jointed by your butcher or fishmonger.

Soak the rabbit pieces for 2–3 hours in fresh water to remove any strong flavour. Pat dry.

Heat the oil in a flameproof casserole. Toss the rabbit pieces in the flour and turn them in the oil until lightly browned, then take out and set aside while softening the onion in the remaining oil. Sprinkle with the rosemary and replace the rabbit pieces. Stir in the calvados, mustard and cider, then cover and simmer very gently for about 30 minutes. Add a little water or stock during cooking as necessary. Season to taste with sea salt and freshly ground pepper.

Serve from the casserole with puréed potatoes and fresh vegetables.

RABBIT STEW

(serves 6)

1 jointed rabbit (a wild one is best)
olive oil for frying
sea salt and pepper
a good tblsp of flour
1 large onion
1 tblsp redcurrant jelly
300 ml/½ pint skimmed milk

Heat a little oil in a pan and brown the meat quickly on all sides. Season and sprinkle with the flour. Tip into a flameproof casserole. Sauté the onion gently in oil, and work the redcurrant jelly into it when it is soft. Add to the rabbit in the casserole. Pour in the milk. Bring to a simmer. Cover, and cook in a slow oven (150°C, Gas Mark 2, 300°F) for 1½ hours.

POLLY'S LAPIN À LA MOUTARDE

(serves 4)

1 young rabbit
2 tblsp Dijon mustard
2 tblsp fresh breadcrumbs
2 tblsp olive oil
2 tsp chopped fresh marjoram
2 tblsp cornflour
300 ml/½ pint white wine
sea salt and freshly ground black pepper
2 tblsp low-fat yogurt

Mix together the mustard, breadcrumbs, oil and marjoram.

Coat the rabbit with this mixture, place in a roasting tin and cook in a moderately hot oven (200°C, Gas Mark 6, 400°F) for 50 minutes, or until tender. Lift the rabbit on to a hot carving dish and keep warm.

Mix the cornflower with a little cold water and pour into the roasting tin with the white wine. Cook gently on top of the cooker for a few minutes, stirring with a wooden spoon. Season, remove from the heat and stir in the yogurt. Strain into a warm sauce boat and serve with the rabbit.

BRAISED PIGEONS

(serves 4)

4 pigeons
225 g/8 oz chopped onions
450 g/1 lb tomatoes, peeled and chopped
sea salt and pepper
fresh thyme or lemon thyme
300 ml/½ pint cider
100 g/4 oz mushrooms
2.5 cm/1 inch cube of fresh ginger, cut into tiny matchsticks
lemon juice and parsley

Wash and dry the pigeons. Lay them in a casserole on the onions and tomatoes. Add seasoning, thyme and cider.

Cover and cook in a slow oven (160°C, Gas Mark 3, 325°F) for 1½ hours.

Half an hour before the end, check that there is enough liquid. Add the shredded ginger and mushrooms.

Before serving, put the pigeons on hot plates. Boil up the juices to reduce them if necessary. Taste for seasoning and add a squeeze of lemon.

Pour the sauce on to the pigeons and sprinkle with parsley.

PIGEONS BAKED IN FOIL

1 pigeon per person
seasoned flour
a little olive oil
a rasher of bacon for each bird
watercress to garnish

Stuffing
mushrooms, fresh breadcrumbs, parsley,
salt and pepper, a little sherry to moisten

Roll the pigeons in flour and brown them lightly in a pan with the olive oil.

Stuff them and put a bacon rasher (cut in half first) on each. Wrap them in cooking foil, sealing the parcel carefully. Put them on a baking sheet and cook in a slow oven (160°C, Gas Mark 3, 325°F) for 1½ hours.

Serve with a jacket potato each, peas and watercress.

Eight
MEAT

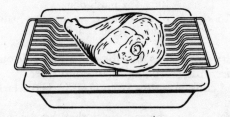

Our native meat, roasted to perfection, is a treat that few of us can resist from time to time – and in a diet that is properly balanced can be indulged in occasionally by even the heart-conscious. Like most 'simple' things it is not at all easy. So here are a few tips on how to develop your skill in achieving perfect results with (usually) expensive raw ingredients. There is nothing more delicious than a beautiful Sunday joint or prime roast fowl giving up its aroma to the house.

It is necessary to say first that the meat you serve will only ever be as good as the meat you buy, so choose a butcher who always sells good meat that has been properly hung. Your oven thermostat must be quite dependable so that you have control over oven temperature. A meat thermometer is a small investment which is well worthwhile. Pushed into the meat towards the end of cooking, it will give you more accuracy in determining whether the roast is pink or medium or well done, whichever way you like it. It takes away some of the guesswork.

The object in roasting is to keep the juices in the joint until it is carved. For this reason it is better not to season meat with salt at the outset of cooking as this causes humidity, which prevents the outside from browning and, by encouraging the juices to run, will toughen and dry out the meat. When needed, only salt the fatty part of the joint. Pepper can get a bit bitter with long cooking so it is better to season at the end.

Never rest the meat on the bottom of the tin. Either place it on a grid or on a bed of chopped vegetables. (Poultry can be laid on its giblets.) This helps to enrich the sauce too.

Use a brush to baste the meat with some olive oil.

The joint is cooked when it is exactly as you like it – a good colour on the outside and juicy and tender inside.

Always allow 10–15 minutes for the meat to 'rest' at the end of cooking in a warm spot such as the warming drawer of the oven or in the oven with the temperature switched right down low and the oven door slightly ajar. The meat is more tender with this treatment, and the juices run less.

ROAST BEEF FILLET

(serves 6)

0.75 kg/1½ lb potatoes
chopped rosemary
olive oil
1.25 kg/2½ lb fillet of beef
150 ml/¼ pint red wine

Cut the peeled potatoes into small chunks and cook them for 4 minutes in boiling salted water. Drain and pat dry. Sprinkle with rosemary and roast in a little oil in a moderately hot oven (200°C, Gas Mark 6, 400°F) for 50 minutes.

Brush the meat with oil and set on a grid in a roasting tin, and roast in the oven below the potatoes, allowing 45–50 minutes, according to taste. After 20 minutes, drain any fat from the tin. Heat the wine, pour it over the meat and continue cooking, basting occasionally.

Pile the potatoes in a small dish. Carve the beef on to a heated serving dish. Strain the juices from the roasting tin and pour them over the meat.

Spinach makes an excellent accompaniment to this dish.

ROAST LEG OF LAMB

(serves 6)

1 1.5 kg/3 lb leg of lamb
3 tblsp olive oil
2 tblsp lemon juice
2 cloves garlic, cut into slivers
1 sprig rosemary
sea salt and freshly ground black pepper

Make several small cuts near the bone with a sharp knife and insert slivers of garlic. Marinate the lamb in the oil and lemon juice for several hours, turning occasionally.

Place the lamb on a grid in a roasting pan and baste with the marinade. Lay the rosemary on top. Roast in a moderately hot oven (200°C, Gas Mark 6, 400°F) for 30 minutes. Baste. Reduce to moderate setting (180°C, Gas Mark 4, 350°F) for a further 1½ hours, basting from time to time. Transfer to a hot carving dish.

Carefully pour away all the fat from the roasting tin, and make a sauce by adding a little stock or wine to the juices in the pan. Season to taste, strain and serve.

ROAST RACK OF LAMB AND RATATOUILLE

(serves 4)

2 joints best end of lamb
(4 cutlets in each), trimmed of fat
2 cloves garlic, crushed
2 sprigs rosemary
2 tblsp sunflower oil
sea salt and freshly ground black pepper

Ask your butcher to chine the joints and remove the horizontal bone, so that the cutlets can be sliced like a loaf of bread. Put the joints of lamb in an oiled roasting tin with the crushed cloves of garlic and sprigs of rosemary underneath. Paint the meat with oil. Place the roasting tin in a pre-heated oven, 200°C, Gas Mark 4, 600°F, for 30 minutes. Sprinkle with sea salt and freshly ground black pepper, carve into cutlets and serve on a bed of ratatouille (see p. 155).

STUFFED SHOULDER OF LAMB

(serves 6)

1 boned shoulder of lamb or tender mutton
weighing 1¼ kg/2½ lb after boning
2 tblsp olive oil
2 sprigs thyme
1 clove of garlic
juice of 1 or 2 oranges
sea salt and pepper

Stuffing
fresh breadcrumbs with a few chopped
soaked dried apricots, sea salt and pepper

Lay out the boned shoulder and stuff the cavity where the bone was removed, then roll it up and tie with string. Do not tie up the meat too tightly as the stuffing swells in the cooking and may burst out untidily.

Rub the rolled meat all over with oil and place it on the thyme and crushed garlic in a roasting tin.

Put the joint into a preheated hot oven, 240°C, Gas Mark 9, 475°F, for 15 minutes. Reduce the heat to 160°C, Gas Mark 3, 325°F, add about 3 tblsp water to the tin and roast for about 1½ hours. After an hour's cooking, baste the joint with orange juice. It makes superb gravy. Tip all the fat away carefully when the meat is cooked.

This is lovely with flageolets or butter beans. You will need about 3 (400g/14oz) tins for 6 people. Heat them, drain and serve with some of the orange-flavoured meat juices. Or use 350g/12oz dried butter beans soaked overnight in cold water, then simmered for 3 hours or until tender in a panful of fresh water. I serve them around the joint, with the meat and orange juices.

This needs no more accompaniment than a crisp salad or a green vegetable.

ROAST FILLET OF LAMB WITH ROSEMARY

(serves 2)

The fillet is that 'eye' of meat that runs along the fairend (also called rack of lamb – or best end). It is remarkably good value as it is lean and tender and sweet. I use it for barbequeing or kebabs – or like this.

1 lamb fillet – about 350 g/12 oz
1 tblsp olive oil
sea salt and black pepper
1 sprig rosemary
1 lemon

Trim the fillet of any bits of sinew. Sprinkle it with a little olive oil and set it aside with the sprig of rosemary to marinate for a little. Set the oven to 200°C, Gas Mark 6, 400°F. Put two jacket potatoes, scrubbed and pricked, into the oven about 1¼ hours before your meal.

Half an hour before serving, set the lamb fillet on the sprig of rosemary in a small roasting tin in the upper part of the oven, above the potatoes. Roast for 25 minutes or until cooked but just pink inside. Rest for 5 minutes in a warm place while you toss a salad. Carve the lamb on to a warm dish and surround with salad. Garnish with a lemon half at each end.

Here is a variation on the dressing for jacket potatoes. Crush 1 tsp coriander seeds. Add to a small carton of low-fat yogurt. Warm together in a little saucepan with a pinch of salt and a few grinds of pepper. To serve the potatoes, cut a cross on the top of each, give them a little squeeze, and pour over the yogurt.

LAMB AND PEPPER KEBABS

(serves 4)

450 g/1 lb fillets of lamb
1 green pepper, deseeded
4 tomatoes, halved
1 small onion, cut in rings
2 tblsp olive oil

Marinade
juice of ½ lemon
1 clove garlic, crushed
sea salt and freshly ground pepper
½ tsp dried oregano
4 tblsp olive oil

Remove any fat from the meat and cut into 2.5cm/1 inch cubes. Cut the flesh of the pepper into small squares. Mix the lemon juice, garlic, seasoning, oregano and oil and pour over the lamb. Marinate for 5–6 hours, turning the meat occasionally.

Thread the lamb, peppers, tomatoes and onion rings on to oiled skewers, and grill or barbecue, turning occasionally, for about 20 minutes. Serve with rice and a tossed salad.

MOUSSAKA

(*serves* 6)

0.5 kg/1 lb aubergines, sliced
1 onion, chopped
2 cloves garlic, crushed
½ tsp dried oregano or marjoram
olive oil to fry
4 tomatoes, peeled and chopped
0.75 kg/1½ lb lean minced lamb
150 ml/¼ pint red wine
bouquet garni
sea salt and freshly ground black pepper
300 ml/½ pint white sauce (see p. 195)
75 g/3 oz low-fat cheese (Edam or Gouda), grated

Sprinkle the aubergines liberally with salt and leave to drain in a colander for an hour. Rinse and pat dry with kitchen paper. Grill on both sides until slightly cooked.

Now make the meat sauce. Fry the onion, garlic and oregano in a little oil until soft. Add the tomatoes, meat and red wine. Stir with a wooden spoon until the grains of meat are separate. Add the bouquet garni and barely simmer, uncovered, for about 15 minutes. Season to taste.

Make up the white sauce.

Now assemble in a large and shallow, greased ovenproof dish. Begin with the meat sauce then aubergine slices and then béchamel sauce. Finally sprinkle with the grated cheese. Cook in a moderate oven (180°C, Gas Mark 4, 350°F) for 45 minutes.

A salad is all you need serve with this satisfying and substantial Greek dish.

LAMB KORMA

(serves 6–8)

A gift of a small assortment of curry spices gave me the push I needed to start experimenting with Indian cooking years ago. Now I like to grind my own spices freshly and add them as they are, or fried in oil or dry roasted. This dish is mild and scented.

1.5 kg/3 lb boneless shoulder or leg of lamb
300 ml/½ pint low-fat yogurt
6 cardamom pods
1 tsp ground cumin seeds
1 tsp ground turmeric
2.5 cm/1 inch cube ginger, peeled and cut small
2 cloves garlic, crushed
¼ tsp cayenne pepper
½ tsp garam masala
100 g/4 oz grated coconut
4 tblsp sunflower oil
2 Spanish onions, peeled and chopped
sea salt and freshly ground black pepper
1 cinnamon stick
4 cloves
4 tomatoes, peeled and quartered
juice of ½ lemon

Trim the meat of any fat and cut it into 2.5 cm/1 inch cubes. Mix the yogurt with the crushed cardamom seeds (peel the cardamom by crushing first, then discard the pod and crush the seeds), the freshly crushed cumin seeds, the ground turmeric, ginger, garlic, cayenne and garam masala. Add the lamb and turn the pieces of meat until well coated. Cover and leave in a cool place for 6 hours.

Simmer the coconut in 300 ml/½ pint water for 15 minutes. Strain the coconut, discard, and keep the strained liquor.

Heat the oil in a frying pan and fry the onions until soft and golden. Add the marinated lamb and yogurt and cook, stirring, for about 5 minutes. Season carefully and mix in the cinnamon stick, cloves, coconut milk and tomatoes. Bring gently back to the boil, cover, and simmer for about 1 hour. Remove the lid if the sauce needs to reduce a little. At the end of the cooking time remove the cinnamon stick and fish out the cloves. Taste for seasoning, add the lemon juice and turn into a hot dish.

Serve with rice and the usual fresh chutneys, salads and side dishes that accompany curry so well: tomato and onion, fresh coriander chutney, poppadoms, etc.

SUMMER RAGOUT OF LAMB

(serves 6)

Start this dish the day before.

1.25 kg/2½ lb boned shoulder of lamb
2 tblsp sunflower oil
1 Spanish onion, peeled and chopped
2 cloves garlic, crushed
2 tblsp flour
sea salt and freshly ground black pepper
2 teaspoons crushed coriander seeds
300 ml/½ pint dry white wine
300 ml/½ pint light stock
6 baby turnips
12 baby carrots
12 little new potatoes
12 shallots or spring onions
225 g/8 oz shelled peas
225 g/8 oz shelled broad beans
a little grated lemon rind

Cut the lamb into 4 cm/1½ inch cubes and trim away the fat. Heat the oil in a large flameproof casserole and brown the lamb. Now remove the meat while you sauté the onion and garlic. Sprinkle with the seasonings (and crushed coriander) and stir until it is all absorbed. Return the lamb pieces to the pan and gradually blend in the wine and stock and bring to the boil. Cover and simmer *gently* for 1 hour. Allow to become cold and then remove all fat from the surface.

Now add the turnips, carrots, potatoes and shallots to the casserole, reheat and simmer for 20 minutes. Put in the peas and broad beans and simmer for another 8–10 minutes.

Serve in hot bowls or plates, sprinkled with lemon rind and chopped parsley.

GRANDMOTHER'S BRAISED STEAK

(serves 4–6)

This takes only a few minutes to prepare, and can then safely be left to cook slowly in a low oven for two hours.

1 tblsp sunflower oil
1 large onion
1 kg/2 lb braising steak
1 tblsp plain flour
400 g/14 oz tin peeled tomatoes
2 tblsp red wine vinegar
2 tsp chopped thyme
sea salt and black pepper

Turn the oven to 150°C, Gas Mark 2, 300°F (if cooking for 2 hours). Alternatively, this dish can be cooked for 3 hours at 130°C, Gas Mark ½, 250°F.

Heat the oil in a heavy pan while you peel and slice the onion. Pass the steak, cut into pieces, through the flour. When the fat is hot, brown the meat on both sides and lay it in a casserole, on a layer of sliced onions. Drain the tomatoes (reserving the juice for soups or sauces) and mix with the wine vinegar, the thyme and some black pepper. Pour this over the meat, cover the pan and cook until tender. Add salt just before serving. You can use wine instead of wine vinegar.

Jacket potatoes can be cooked at the same time as the meat and are an excellent accompaniment.

CASSEROLE OF BEEF WITH WINE

(serves 6)

1 kg/2 lb lean braising steak
2 tblsp olive oil
2 large onions, chopped
2 cloves garlic, crushed
50 g/2 oz lean smoked bacon, diced
1 tblsp flour
sea salt and freshly ground black pepper
½ tsp chopped thyme
300 ml/½ pint dry red wine
1 tblsp tomato purée, diluted with a little water

Cut the beef into 4 cm/1½ inch cubes. Heat the oil in a large, thick-bottomed casserole and fry the onion and garlic until golden. Add the bacon and cook for a few minutes. Stir in the flour and then add the beef, combining all well together. Season lightly and add the remaining ingredients. Cover and bring slowly back to the boil.

Transfer to a cool oven (150°C, Gas Mark 2, 300°F) for 2 hours, until tender. Reduce the heat after 1 hour of cooking if the casserole is bubbling more than very gently. Adjust the seasoning and serve from the casserole.

BOILED BEEF AND CARROTS

(serves 8)

A very old-fashioned and comforting dish.

2.5 kg/5 lb silverside pickled beef (corned)
6 medium carrots
1 medium onion
1 clove
2 large onions
2 small turnips
bouquet garni (1 bayleaf, 1 sprig thyme,
6 black peppercorns, 8 parsley stalks,
3 inch celery)
sea salt and freshly ground pepper

Completely cover the meat in cold water and soak for 1 hour. Tie the bouquet garni in a piece of cloth. Stick the clove into the medium onion. Cut the carrots into quarters. Roughly cut up the turnips. Slice the large onions.

Pour off the water in which the meat has been soaking, as this will be rather salty.

Place the meat in a large pot and cover with cold water and bring it up to boiling point. Pour off this water and cover once again with fresh, cold water. Pop in the bouquet garni. When the 'stock' has come to the boil reduce the heat and allow to simmer for 1¼ hours, skimming frequently.

After this period of cooking, remove the bouquet garni and add the roughly cut vegetables and the onion containing the clove. Bring to the boil. Skim and continue to simmer for a further 30 minutes.

Check that the meat is tender, remove it from the stock and place on a warmed serving dish. Surround the meat with the vegetables. Skim the stock and serve it in a sauceboat.

This is traditional fare. Served on blue and white china with boiled potatoes and chopped parsley, it looks and tastes wonderful.

OLD ENGLISH CASSEROLE OF BEEF

(serves 6)

1 kg/2 lb shin of beef
flour to toss
4 large carrots
3 tblsp olive oil
18 shallots
1 tsp dry mustard
1 tsp chopped herbs
450 ml/¾ pint beef stock
225 g/½ lb button mushrooms
sea salt and freshly ground black pepper

Trim any fat and gristle from the beef and cut the meat into 2 cm/¾ inch cubes. Toss them in the flour. Roughly chop the carrots.

Heat the oil in a large casserole and brown the meat rapidly on all sides. Take out and set aside. Add the carrots and shallots to the pan and cook for a few minutes over a low heat, stirring with a wooden spoon. When the vegetables are golden, remove and put with the meat. Sprinkle the mustard and herbs on to the remaining oil and pan juices and stir well. Gradually blend in the stock. Return the meat and vegetables to the pan and add seasoning to taste. Heat through and cover tightly.

Cook in a cool oven (150°C, Gas Mark 2, 300°F) for 2 hours, until the meat is tender, adding the mushrooms 20 minutes before the end.

JUMPY

He appeared quite suddenly in the open doorway of the restaurant kitchen. His silhouette made me look up from what I was doing. 'Hello,' he said, 'I'm Jumpy.' He was a young Indian, slender and nice-looking. I couldn't remember having seen him before.

He put a sheaf of handwritten notes on the counter top and left as quickly as he had come. He had written an account of the origins of a beef curry as well as its recipe. Squiggly diagrams and drawings in the recipe itself showed pieces of ginger, garlic and chillies actual size; sadly I cannot reproduce them here. There was a stick of cinnamon there too and a skimming spoon, suitable shapes and sizes for saucepans, ideal thickness of tomato and onion slices and much more besides. This was some years ago now and I still really treasure this document.

This is how it goes:

'Dear Beth,

A curry is one of the most class-conscious dishes in the world. The poor cook it very quickly (because of the high cost of fuel) and make it very hot (because the meat is usually off in the hotter parts of the country). This is what the soldiers in India ate. The box-wallahs (traders) and civil servants had more opportunity to eat curries with the richer folks. It is one of these that I will describe.

You must understand Hindus don't eat meat so a beef curry of high quality could only come from a rich Muslim or Anglo-Indian family. It tends to be more primitive than a Parsi beef curry in that it still resembles the quick-cook and hot variety. The Parsi one which is described below is mild and should release several tastes progressively in the eating of it. Homogeneity of taste is a mark of failure.

JUMPY'S BEEF CURRY

(serves 4)

1 tblsp coriander seeds
1 tblsp cumin seeds
½ tblsp garam masala
1 tsp huldi (turmeric)
¼ tsp sugar
4 garlic cloves, crushed
4 cm/1½ inch piece ginger, crushed
2 green chilli peppers, chopped
2 large onions, chopped
sunflower oil and butter for frying
675 g/1½ lb beef, cubed
4 medium-sized, ripe tomatoes, skinned and chopped
15 cm/2 inch stick of cinnamon
1 aubergine
sea salt and black pepper to taste
desiccated coconut to make coconut milk

Optional
fresh cream
roasted almonds or cashew nuts

Grind the spices in a pestle and mortar or a blender. Gently fry the garlic, ginger, chilli peppers and onions in oil and butter until pale and soft. Add the ground spices and fry a little longer. Don't let it burn.

Now add the beef and fry very gently until the outside is lightly browned but soggy.

Chop up the aubergine into small dice. This gives texture and helps absorb taste. Then add one can of tomatoes. Better of course to chop up 4 medium-sized tomatoes. (Worst of all is to use tomato purée. You see, tomato purée burns quickly and its stickiness causes everything else to cook unevenly.)

Now drop in a stick of cinnamon. Keep stirring to this point. Leave it cooking very gently for about an hour or until the meat is tender. The meat should not arrive at the table overdone. The longer and slower you cook it the better it is. It also means that the curry will be thick while the texture of the aubergine is only discernible to an acute observer and taster.

Important note: If left cold for a few hours and then reheated before serving, the taste will be much better.

You can add water with the tomatoes and then later thicken it with desiccated coconut. This way it has a creamier texture.

You could go the whole hog (cow) and do a royal beef pasanda by thickening it with fresh cream before serving and sprinkling chopped almonds and cashew nuts on top.

The rice

Nothing is better than American-grown Basmati rice. Then comes Patna rice, long grain. After that Patna rice from chain stores and last of all that foul fluffy concoction, 'easy-to-cook'.

Wash rice at least five times in lukewarm water while rubbing it between your hands. The last wash should give off only slightly cloudy water.

Judge the amount of water – this comes with practice – and add salt.

Boil up to foaming and skim off foam with a skimming spoon. Place lid askew and boil on the gentlest of heat in a heavy saucepan. At this point leave rice after inserting a couple of sticks of cinnamon and ½ tblsp butter.

Salad

Chop onions into fine slices, wash a couple of times (just like the rice) to remove bitterness. Chop tomatoes and cucumber, also finely. Add vinegar and salt to taste. Sprinkle lightly with paprika.

Good luck.

Jumpy'

CASSOULET
(*serves 10*)

This is a famous French provincial dish. It is a rich stew with more than one sort of meat and a spicy sausage, slow-cooked with beans. In France it is usually enriched with preserved neck of goose. At home I often make it with lamb, either shoulder or fillet. A good powerful continental sausage is vital.

This recipe is not authentic, but is my adaptation for using our own local ingredients. It makes a really hearty meal, and calls for nothing else but some crusty bread and a simple green salad.

This dish reheats like a dream.

450 g/1 lb mixed haricot beans and green lentils
600 ml/1 pint good home-made stock
3 celery sticks, chopped
2 carrots, finely chopped
3 leeks, chopped
1 large Spanish onion, peeled and chopped
3 tblsp tomato purée
1 bay leaf
450 g/1 lb topside of beef
350 g/12 oz neck fillet of lamb
100 g/4 oz spicy, garlicky French sausage
or smoked bacon, chopped
plenty of fresh thyme, pulled off its stalks
1 glass red wine
2 tblsp olive oil
3 cloves garlic, crushed
4 ripe tomatoes, peeled, deseeded and chopped
175 g/6 oz peas
sea salt and black pepper, to taste

Put the pulses to soak in water the night before. The next day drain them and put them into a large casserole with the beef stock and bring this gently to the boil. Add the celery, carrots, leeks, onion, tomato purée and bay leaf. Cover and simmer very gently for about an hour, adding more water if necessary. Skim off any scum.

Meanwhile trim the beef and lamb of all visible fat and cut them into chunks.

Add the meat to the casserole, with the sausage (or bacon), thyme and wine.

Now put the casserole into a preheated oven, 150°C, Gas Mark 2, 300°F, for 3–3½ hours or until meat and pulses are tender.

Near the end of the cooking time, fry the garlic gently in olive oil and add the tomatoes and peas.

Take out the casserole and add this last mixture. Season carefully with as little salt as possible and plenty of freshly ground black pepper. Keep warm in a low oven.

PORC À L'ORANGE

(serves 6)

1.25 kg/2½ lb pork fillet
2 tblsp seasoned flour
2 tblsp sunflower oil
a little chopped thyme
300 ml/½ pint chicken stock
juice of 2 oranges
juice of 1 lemon
2 tblsp orange liqueur
2 tblsp demerara sugar
sea salt and freshly ground black pepper
orange slices to garnish

Cut the pork fillet into small escalopes 2 cm/¾ inch thick and toss in seasoned flour. Heat the oil in a large pan and gently fry the pork with the thyme until tender. Transfer to a hot serving dish and keep warm.

Add the chicken stock to the meat juices in the pan, then stir in the fruit juices, liqueur and sugar. Bring to the boil, stirring, then simmer without a lid until reduced by half. Season, strain over the pork and garnish with orange slices.

PORC AUX PRUNEAUX

(serves 4)

This is adapted from Curnonsky's *Recettes des Provinces de France*. The dish is made with pork fillet, the prunes that are so exquisitely displayed in the shop windows in Tours, and the local delicious wine of the Loire, Vouvray.

0.5 kg/1 lb giant prunes
½ bottle Vouvray or medium dry white wine
675 g/1½ lb pork fillet
2 tblsp seasoned flour
1 tblsp sunflower oil
2 tsp redcurrant jelly
sea salt and freshly ground black pepper
300 ml/½ pint low-fat yogurt
chopped parsley to garnish

Soak the prunes overnight in the wine.

Cut the pork fillet into cubes and turn in the seasoned flour. Fry gently on all sides in the oil until golden and cooked through.

Meanwhile, simmer the prunes for 30 minutes in the wine. Drain and place around the edge of a heated serving dish. Arrange the pork in the centre. Add the prune liquor to the meat juices in the frying pan, boil to reduce slightly and thicken, then stir in the redcurrant jelly until blended. Taste for and adjust seasoning. Carefully stir half the yogurt into it and warm through. Pour it over the pork, but not the prunes, and spoon the remaining yogurt over. Garnish with parsley and serve with a watercress and tomato salad.

PORK CREOLE STYLE

(*serves* 6)

1.5 kg/3 lb tenderloin of pork
3 tblsp flour
4 tblsp sunflower oil
1 large Spanish onion, peeled and chopped
2 cloves garlic, crushed
1 kg/2 lb tomatoes, peeled and deseeded
2 small chilli peppers, sliced
twist of lemon peel
1 tblsp curry powder
1 bay leaf
2 tblsp freshly chopped thyme
600 ml/1 pint light stock
sea salt and pepper
300 ml/½ pint low-fat yogurt
1 tblsp cornflour
freshly chopped parsley to garnish

Trim the meat, discarding any fat, and cut into 4 cm/1½ inch cubes. Dust with the flour. Heat the oil in a flameproof casserole and brown the pork all over. Remove the meat and cook the onion and garlic until softened. Return the meat to the casserole with the tomatoes, chillies, lemon peel, curry powder, bay leaf, thyme and stock. Cover and simmer gently for 1 hour. Season to taste and cook for a further hour.

Just before serving, mix the yogurt with the cornflour and stir into the meat mixture. Cook, stirring, for a few minutes. Dust the top with parsley and serve with rice.

SALTIMBOCCA

(serves 4)

The name literally means 'jump into the mouth' (it is *so* good!).

8 slices raw smoked ham
8 small sage leaves
8 thin slices veal fillet
flour to coat
1 tblsp olive oil
150 ml/¼ pint Marsala or sherry
twist of lemon peel
salt and freshly ground black pepper
lemon slices and sage leaves to garnish

Place the slice of ham and a sage leaf on each veal fillet. Roll up and tie with cotton. Coat the rolls lightly with flour.

Heat the oil in a frying pan. Put in the veal olives and cook on all sides until they start to turn golden. Pour in the Marsala or sherry and add the lemon peel. Simmer gently for about 10 minutes, season to taste, and serve on a hot dish with the sauce spooned over.

Garnish with the lemon slices and sage leaves.

ITALIAN VEAL CASSEROLE

(serves 6)

6 slices shin of veal (each 5cm/2 inches thick)
or 0.75 kg/1½ lb pie veal
3 tblsp olive oil
seasoned flour to coat
150 ml/¼ pint dry white wine
1 Spanish onion, finely chopped
0.75 kg/1½ lb tomatoes, peeled and roughly chopped
1 tsp chopped lemon thyme
150 ml/¼ pint light stock
sea salt and freshly ground black pepper
1 lemon
1 clove garlic, crushed
2 tblsp chopped parsley

Shin of veal is the traditional flavoursome cut used for this dish. If using pie veal, trim and cube.

Heat the oil in a heavy-bottomed flameproof casserole. Cook the veal, lightly dusted with the seasoned flour, until golden. If using shin, stand the veal upright, so the marrow does not fall out of the bone. Add the wine, onion, tomatoes, herbs, stock and seasoning. Bring to simmering point, cover and cook gently for 1½–2 hours. Take off the lid after the first hour if the sauce needs reducing.

Grate the rind of the lemon and mix with the garlic and parsley. Sprinkle this over the casserole just before serving. Italian risotto rice, coloured with a pinch of saffron which has been steeped in a few tablespoons of boiling water, goes well with this marvellous dish.

HUNGARIAN VEAL GOULASH

(serves 6–8)

Originally cooked by shepherds in a pot over an open fire, the gulyás (goulash) later became adapted to the sophisticated tastes of the Hapsburg court. Today the gulyás can be a glorious spicy stew or a delicately flavoured dish fit for an archduke! Traditional accompaniments are buttered noodles, lescó (a spicy ratatouille made with bacon and paprika), long-grain rice, and little balls of cucumber which have been sautéed in oil, bathed in warm yogurt and dusted with salt and pepper.

1.75 kg/4 lb breast of veal
5 tblsp sunflower oil
1 large onion, peeled and chopped
1 clove garlic, crushed
2 tblsp flour, seasoned with sea salt and pepper
2 tblsp paprika
4 medium tomatoes, peeled, deseeded and chopped
1 green pepper, deseeded and diced
1 glass white wine
1 tsp sea salt
1½ tsp cornflour
450 ml/¾ pint low-fat yogurt
freshly chopped parsley to garnish

Trim the veal of all fat, skin and tissue. Heat the oil in a flameproof casserole and sauté the onion and garlic. Cut the veal into 2.5 cm/1 inch cubes, toss them in the flour and stir into the onion, continuing to sauté for about 10 minutes. Add the paprika and mix well. Stir in the tomatoes, green pepper and salt. Pour in a little wine to almost cover. Place a lid on the casserole and continue to simmer very gently for 1 hour. Check occasionally to see that the liquid has not evaporated, and give the meat a stir. Add a little water if necessary.

Mix the cornflour with a little of the yogurt and then add the rest of the yogurt. Pour this gradually into the gulyás, stirring, and simmer for a minute or two. Heat carefully, but do not boil. Dust with parsley to serve.

Nine

VEGETABLES AND SALADS

'Luscious, tempting vegetables', said the seventeenth-century diarist John Evelyn, and most of us would still agree with that.

When buying vegetables of any kind, don't forget that fresh is always best. If you are in a hurry the simplest way of cooking them is to use a steamer: this keeps more of the natural goodness locked into the vegetables themselves instead of it disappearing into the cooking water. Steamed vegetables – cooked until just 'al dente' – also retain their colour better and look more appetising.

Onions, shallots, leeks, garlic and chives are basic to our cooking and it is difficult to imagine being without them. They are practically national emblems in France and Spain (and in Bermuda too, I gather). Gently fried onions and garlic form the base flavouring of so many dishes, soups, casseroles and sauces. I always associate the smell of onions and sweet peppers frying with the book *The Godfather*. In times of trouble (when they 'took the mattresses') Mama was in the kitchen preparing a meal and the house was filled with the familiar, soothing and promising aroma.

Shallots are a kind of onion, but form a cluster of bulbs rather than a single bulb. They are invaluable for sauces.

Chives are the delicate green shoots we use in salads and sauces.

Leeks are a subtle and delicious vegetable and need no explaining. A leek is a good addition to any fish soup. It is also the basis of ever popular leek and potato soup.

Garlic is the subject of much heated disagreement. You love it or you hate it. It is strong and pungent, with such a profuse odour that 'one merely needs to rub the soles of one's feet with it in order to make one's breath reek offensively of garlic'. This odour may be the reason for its long association with the devil, and the belief that vampires are repulsed by garlic. Gardeners underplant roses with garlic to ward off greenfly, and now scientists have evolved time-release capsules which, planted under forest trees, give them garlic 'breath' to repel animals which damage the trees.

Years ago it was a country practice to include plenty of wild garlic in salads and sandwiches in order to cleanse and purify the blood. Doctors and scientists have long believed in its health-giving properties. Certain extracts of garlic are antibacterial and antifungal; other extracts are antithrombotic – they inhibit the clotting of blood and are good for circulatory disorders.

STIR-FRY VEGETABLES

This attractive and quick way of cooking comes from Chinese wok cookery. The crispness, colour and flavour are locked in by very quick frying. Combine almost any vegetables that you please and cut them into fine strips that take no more than 3 minutes to cook. Broccoli, Chinese cabbage, carrot, celery, leeks, button mushrooms, red and green sweet peppers, bean sprouts, cabbage and courgettes are all suitable. Use olive oil for frying them as it withstands high temperatures best.

Prepare the vegetables and have them ready. Heat 2 table-spoons of oil in a wok or a large frying pan and stir-fry your vegetables fast in this until they are just cooked but still crunchy.

Tofu can be added for protein, or blanched almonds (fried for a few moments before adding to the vegetables) or cashew nuts.

Soy sauce can be shaken in at the end of cooking for extra flavour, and garlic and little strips of fresh ginger (cut like matchsticks) give a lovely oriental taste.

VEGETABLES BAKED IN THE OVEN

Try baking whole, scrubbed parsnips in the oven. They cook just like baked potatoes, and are really sweet and delicious split open and sprinkled with a little pepper and salt. You can take the experiment further by baking whole onions in their skins too. Turn out the inside of the onion on to your plate, discarding the outer, brown skin, and enjoy the mild succulent onion with all its goodness and flavour intact. If you are avoiding butter you could try the way I do it, serving a sauce of yogurt, freshly chopped herbs and a little crushed garlic.

A yen for something spicy can be satisfied by briefly sautéing in a small pan with a little olive oil a crushed clove of garlic with a chopped chilli pepper and matchsticks of fresh ginger, which you spoon over the vegetables as an alternative to the yogurt sauce.

Whole aubergines can be baked in the oven until soft. Prick them first and give them 35 minutes in a moderately hot oven. Then make a wonderful purée by scooping the flesh out into a blender and dribbling oil and lemon juice in through the 'feed'. Add finely chopped onion (about half an onion to 3 or 4 aubergines). Don't blend this but add it by hand. Season well and set aside for a few hours before using. Simply eat with chunks of good bread.

Courgettes can be simply cooked by splitting them lengthwise and laying them in a shallow, covered dish, cut side up, with a spoonful or two of water, lemon juice and a sprinkling of oil. Season lightly and bake in a moderate oven for about 30 minutes. Halved tomatoes are delicious when put alongside the courgettes in the same dish. Serve with a generous dusting of chopped fresh herbs.

BRAISED CELERY

(serves 4)

Fennel can be treated in the same way. Serve as a first course, or as an accompaniment to fish and meat dishes.

2 heads celery
300 ml/½ pint stock
7 g/¼ oz butter

Trim and rinse the celery. Cut each head in four and blanch in boiling salted water for 5 minutes. Drain thoroughly.

Place the celery in a shallow ovenproof dish, pour the stock over it and dot with butter. Cover the dish with a lid or foil and cook in a moderately hot oven (190°C, Gas Mark 5, 375°F) for 20–30 minutes, until tender.

COURGETTES
(serves 4)

0.75 kg/1½ lb courgettes, sliced
3 tblsp olive oil
1 clove garlic, crushed
juice of ½ lemon
sea salt and freshly ground black pepper
torn basil leaves to garnish

Fry the courgettes in oil with the garlic, lemon juice and pepper, turning once, until they are soft and golden brown. Season with salt, sprinkle with basil and serve.

N.B.   Add some peeled, deseeded and roughly chopped tomatoes to the courgettes to make courgettes Provençale.

STUFFED CABBAGE
(serves 4)

Very tempting and plenty of fibre!

8–10 green cabbage leaves
a little sunflower oil
1 small onion, chopped
1 clove garlic, chopped
450 g/1 lb lean minced beef
100 g/4 oz cooked brown rice
½ tsp ground cinnamon
2–3 tblsp low-fat yogurt
freshly ground black pepper and a little sea salt

Sauce
600 ml/1 pint tomato juice
1 tblsp cornflower dissolved in 3 tblsp water
rind of ½ orange (optional)
freshly ground black pepper and a little sea salt

Remove the hard stalks from the cabbage leaves. Trim the leaves so that you have good-sized pieces to wrap the filling in. Blanch the leaves for 2–3 minutes in boiling water. Drain and dry. Set aside.

Next make the filling. Heat the oil in a large pan. Add the onion, garlic and meat. Cook for 3–4 minutes. Stir into this the cooked rice, cinnamon, yogurt, seasoning and 2–3 tblsp of the tomato juice from the sauce. Mix the lot together well. Lay the cabbage leaves out flat. Place a spoonful of the filling on each leaf. Wrap up neatly to form a parcel. Place in a shallow baking dish.

Set oven 180°C, Gas Mark 4, 350°F.

Heat the juice in a saucepan. Add the dissolved cornflour, orange rind and seasoning. When the sauce comes to the boil and has begun to thicken slightly, pour it over the parcels. Cover the dish with a lid or foil and bake for 40 minutes. Serve with crusty wholemeal bread, jacket or boiled potatoes to complete the meal.

GLOBE ARTICHOKES

(serves 4)

This is how to prepare them 'au naturel' – or perfectly simply.

4 globe artichokes,
weighing about 350 g/12 oz each
½ lemon
4 litres/7 pints water
1 tblsp sea salt

Trim the bases of the artichokes so that they will sit flat on a plate. Snap and pull off the bottom leaves all around. Put each artichoke on its side and cut a good 2.5 cm/1 inch off the top with a sharp knife or a bread knife. Rub any cut edges with lemon to stop them discolouring.

Put the artichokes into a large pan and add enough water so that it's about an inch deep.

Squeeze the rest of the lemon into the water. Bring to the boil, add salt, then reduce the heat and steam, covered, for 15 to 20 minutes. At the end of this time try plucking one of the top leaves. If it comes off easily the artichokes are ready.

Take them out of the pan, invert and leave to drain for a minute or two. Grasp the 'choke' in the middle of each and pull it out gently and firmly. Discard.

Serve the artichokes cold with vinaigrette, i.e. oil and vinegar with seasoning and a little chopped shallot and fresh herbs. Or you may like them with mayonnaise.

Artichokes should be eaten with the fingers, and it is pleasant to give each person a finger bowl – a small bowl of warm water with a little lemon in it – and a napkin to dry their hands with afterwards.

BAKED BEETROOT
(serves 4)

8–10 baby beetroots, washed but not peeled
juice and a little grated rind of 1 orange
2 tsp cornflour
300 ml/½ pint low-fat yogurt
¼ tsp caraway seeds
a little sea salt and black pepper

Boil the beetroots gently until tender, or cook them in a pressure cooker for about 15 minutes. Let them cool a little while you mix together the orange juice, rind and the cornflour. Stir this into the yogurt. Crush the caraway seeds and stir them in too, seasoning with a little salt and pepper.

Peel the beetroots and slice them. Add to the orangey yogurt and put into a covered dish in the oven at 200°C, Gas Mark 5, 375°F for about 20 minutes or half an hour.

POTATOES ANNA
(serves 4–6)

This is particularly suitable for new potatoes.

Grease an ovenproof dish. Cut the potatoes into rings about 0.3cm/⅛ inch thick. Arrange them to fill the dish. Add salt and pepper (just a little) and several small knobs of butter with each layer, then pour half a cup of skimmed milk over.

Bake for 1 hour with the lid on at 190°C, Gas Mark 5, 375°F. Then take the lid off and give them another 30 minutes (turn the oven down a little if they seem to be going too fast).

This dish will keep happily in a low oven until you are ready.

POMMES LYONNAISE

(serves 4–6)

Put evenly and thinly sliced potatoes into a shallow dish with some chopped onion. Pour in stock to almost cover. Brush the top with a little oil. Cover with foil and bake in a medium-hot oven (190°C, Gas Mark 5, 375°F) for an hour, or until done.

RICED POTATOES

Plain boiled potatoes are made into a lovely light snow by an old-fashioned gadget, obtainable from most caterers' suppliers and some kitchen shops, called simply a potato ricer.

Use the ricer for cooked swedes as well. Mix the riced swedes with a little crushed garlic, and season well with sea salt and freshly ground black pepper. Add a little butter. Not a bit like school veg!

POMMES BOULANGÈRE

(serves 4)

So called because in France this potato dish used to be taken along to the bakery with the joint of meat, to be popped into the big oven when it was still hot but cooling down after baking the day's batch of bread. It is best cooked when you have the oven on anyway for a joint of meat or a casserole.

1 kg/2 lb potatoes
1 clove garlic
salt and black pepper
50 g/2 oz butter

Peel the potatoes and slice them very thinly, about the thickness of a coin.

Rub the inside of the dish with the cut clove of garlic. (You will need a good ovenproof dish with a lid.)

Arrange the potato slices in layers with dots of butter and a little salt and pepper between each layer. Use all the potatoes like this. Dot the top with butter and cover with a piece of greaseproof paper. Put on the lid. Bake in a moderate oven (190°C, Gas Mark 5, 350°F) for 45 minutes to an hour, or longer if the oven is lower or if you have a joint above the potatoes.

Remove the lid and the greaseproof paper for the last 15 minutes – or brown under the grill before serving.

ROSTI

(serves 6)

This is so good – and an excellent accompaniment to meat, game and fish.

1 kg/2 lb potatoes, peeled
2 tblsp sunflower oil
sea salt and pepper

Partly cook the potatoes for 10 minutes, drain and cool. Chill in the fridge for several hours or overnight. This is important for the texture of the rosti.

Grate the potatoes with a coarse grater. Season with salt and pepper. Heat the oil in a non-stick frying pan and put in the potato in an even layer. Pat the potato down gently and cook slowly for 10 minutes or until the underside is golden. Shuffle the pan frequently as the potato is cooking so that it doesn't stick.

Now flip over the potato cake (just as you would a pancake). Fry until the second side is golden. Place an inverted hot dish on top and turn out the rosti on to it by turning over together the pan and the dish. Cut into slices and serve.

RATATOUILLE PROVENCALE

2 aubergines, cubed
2 large onions, peeled and chopped
6 tblsp olive oil
2 cloves garlic, crushed
3 green peppers, deseeded and diced
4 courgettes, sliced
8 ripe tomatoes, peeled and chopped
chopped fresh marjoram or oregano
sea salt and freshly ground black pepper
1 tsp sugar
1 tsp crushed coriander seeds
1 black olive to garnish

Put the aubergines in a colander with a sprinkling of salt and leave to drain for 30 minutes. Rinse and pat dry in kitchen paper.

Soften the onions in olive oil, then add the garlic, aubergines and the rest of the vegetables. Add the chopped herbs (use thyme if you have neither of the others), seasoning, sugar and coriander seeds. Cover and simmer gently for a further 20–30 minutes, stirring from time to time.

Serve hot with bread, or serve cold as a salad or a starter, on a lettuce leaf, and garnished with a black olive.

CHINESE SALAD

(serves 6)

It is impossible to plan a salad to the last detail as the only unbreakable rule is that all ingredients should be the freshest available. The following salad is composed with an eye to textures, tastes and appearance – don't feel tied to the ingredients.

1 head Chinese leaves
⅓ cucumber, thinly sliced
1 avocado pear
1 ripe eating pear
juice of ½ lemon
1 bunch watercress

Dressing
150 ml/¼ pint yogurt
1 tsp tomato purée (or 2 tsp tomato ketchup)
½ tsp paprika
2 tblsp freshly chopped chives
a little sea salt and fresh pepper
2 tsp wine vinegar
3 tblsp warm water

Cut some of the Chinese leaves into a bowl (cover the rest and put in the fridge for sandwiches or salad lunch tomorrow). Add the cucumber. The avocado must be ripe – and not over-ripe;

it should be just soft to the touch when pressed with the thumb. Halve, remove the stone, peel and slice into a small bowl. Peel, core and slice the dessert pear and add to the avocado. Turn them gently in the lemon juice (to prevent them from discolouring). Wash the watercress and throw the sprigs (not too much stalk) into the Chinese leaves.

Combine the dressing ingredients in the order listed, working in the warm water well. Store the dressing in a jar (it will keep for a week) and use only as much as you want.

Toss all the salad together *just* before serving – this is important – with its dressing.

MUSHROOM AND BEAN SALAD
WITH HAZELNUT DRESSING

(serves 6)

This is one of my favourites. It can also be served as a starter.

225 g/8 oz French beans, cut into chunks
225 g/8 oz button mushrooms
1 head crisp lettuce
25 g/1 oz roasted, chopped hazelnuts

Hazelnut dressing
4 tblsp sunflower oil
2 tblsp hazelnut oil
1 tblsp cider or wine vinegar
1 tsp sugar
sea salt and pepper
1 tsp Dijon mustard

Mix all the dressing ingredients together.

Simmer the beans in a little water until just cooked but still crisp. Drain and refresh with ice-cold water. Slice the mushrooms and put in the bowl with the cooked beans, spoon some hazelnut dressing over and leave for the flavours to blend for an hour or two.

Slice the lettuce into a fine chiffonade (ribbons) and arrange a bed on each of 6 individual plates. Pile a mound of beans and mushrooms on to each and sprinkle with chopped hazelnuts before serving.

SALAD WITH WALNUTS

(serves 6)

2 sticks celery, cut into small pieces
2 apples, cored and cubed but not peeled
3 endives, chopped into bite-sized pieces
75 g/3 oz whole walnuts
6 good-sized lettuce leaves
3 avocados
small sprigs of watercress
25 g/1 oz chopped walnuts for garnish

Dressing
5 tblsp mayonnaise (see p. 192)
3 tblsp yogurt
2 tsp curry powder

Mix together the celery, apples, endive and walnuts in a bowl. Place a large attractive lettuce leaf on each of six plates. Halve, peel and slice the avocado pears and lay each half in a fan around the lettuce leaf. Put a small bunch of watercress sprigs on each plate too.

Mix the dressing ingredients together with a whisk in a large bowl. To this add the apple salad mixture and whole walnuts and toss until well coated.

Spoon salad on to each lettuce leaf and add chopped walnuts in a little pile on the top.

Delicious either as an accompaniment to a main course or as a starter.

COLESLAW

(serves 8)

1 small white cabbage
2 Cox's apples
juice of 1 lemon
1 head celery
2 tblsp chopped parsley
2 tblsp snipped chives
1 red sweet pepper, deseeded and finely chopped
French dressing (see pp. 188–9)
150 ml/¼ pint low-fat yogurt

Shred the cabbage finely, discarding the tough white stalk. Core and chop the apples (leaving the skin on) and toss them in the lemon juice. Wash and chop the celery, using the tender inside leaves and stalks. Place the cabbage, apples, celery and remaining ingredients in a large bowl. Pour over them enough French dressing and yogurt to coat and toss all together well.

CARROT SALAD
(*serves 4*)

The sweet, bright carrot is an underrated vegetable. It could hardly be more versatile in its uses, making salads, variously accompanying main courses, going into soups, sauces and stews, into cakes (the main ingredient of passion cake is carrot!), and even into the Christmas pudding. Children love them, which is more than can be said of most vegetables.

450 g/1 lb carrots, grated
1 bulb of fennel, grated
juice of 1 orange
sea salt and pepper

Mix all these together, tasting for enough salt (not too much). Chill in a glass bowl, turn over and mix the salad again and serve.

CARROT AND ORANGE SALAD
(*serves 10*)

450 g/1 lb carrots, washed and grated
juice of 2 oranges
2 tblsp raisins
sea salt and freshly ground pepper
fresh coriander leaves (or parsley, chopped)

Toss all together. This is both beautiful and good.

CARROT AND APPLE SALAD

(serves 6)

A refreshing and satisfying salad with a hint of warm coriander spice.

450g/1lb carrots, scrubbed and coarsely grated
juice of 1 lemon
2 tsp Dijon mustard
1 tsp coriander seeds, crushed
2 tblsp apple juice
2 dessert apples, cored and chopped
sea salt and black pepper
3 tblsp chopped parsley

Put the grated carrots into a bowl. Whisk together the lemon juice, mustard, crushed coriander seeds and apple juice. Turn the apples in this, season with salt and pepper and fold together with the parsley.

Turn the apple mixture into the bowl of grated carrot and stir everything together. Taste again for seasoning.

TOMATO SALAD

I always make tomato salad in one of three ways, all absolutely delicious.

1 Peel and slice tomatoes.
   Sprinkle them with olive oil, sea salt, black pepper.
   Top with chopped, fresh mint.

2 Peel and slice tomatoes.
   Add sea salt and black pepper.
   Strew with fresh basil.
   Sprinkle with a little olive oil.

3 Peel and slice tomatoes.
   Slice onion rings really finely and soak them in cold water.
   Drain the onion rings and strew them over the tomatoes.
   Add sea salt and black pepper.
   Sprinkle with a few drops of olive oil.
   Add a dusting of chopped parsley.
   And, sometimes, chopped black olives.

TOMATO AND AVOCADO SALAD

(serves 2)

1 ripe avocado
1 large ripe beef tomato
a few black olives
2 tsp lemon juice
2 tblsp olive oil
sea salt and black pepper

Halve the avocado, skin it and remove the stone. Put the halves, cut side down, on to 2 plates. Slice them downwards into strips, then press them slightly with the flat of your hand to fan them out. Slice the tomato and arrange half on each plate (in a fan beside the avocado). Put the olives on the side. Sprinkle lemon juice on to the avocado and olive oil on to the tomato. Season with a little salt and plenty of freshly ground black pepper.

Serve with a wholemeal roll or a chunk of good bread.

TUNA SALAD

(serves 2)

1 crisp lettuce heart
1 198g/7oz can tuna fish, drained
100g/4oz fromage frais
freshly ground pepper
¼ tsp celery salt
½ tsp curry powder
1 onion, peeled and sliced into rings
2 tomatoes, peeled and quartered
50g/2oz black olives
2 tblsp French dressing (see p. 188)

Arrange the washed lettuce leaves on two plates. Mash the tuna with the yogurt and season with the pepper, celery salt and curry powder. Heap a mound of this mixture on to each plate. Scatter onion rings over all and dot with the tomato quarters and olives. Finally trickle a little French dressing over the lettuce surrounding the fish.

TUNA FISH AND BEAN SALAD

This is a simpler variation on the above but just as delicious.

Drain tinned tuna fish and mix with haricot beans which have been soaked overnight and cooked for 2 to 2½ hours (or use tinned ones).

Lay onion rings on this salad and dress with a squeeze of lemon juice, a little olive oil, seasoning and dusting of parsley.

SALAD OF MACKEREL NIÇOISE

(serves 4)

4 fillets of mackerel
100 g/4 oz French beans
2 small lettuce hearts
4 tomatoes, skinned
1 shallot (or spring onions), peeled
12 black olives
olive oil
lemon juice
sea salt and black pepper

Get the grill bars really hot. Lay the mackerel on them, skin side upwards. Grill for a few minutes under a moderate heat. Strip off the skin, turn the fillets over and grill for a few minutes more.

Top and tail the beans and steam them until they are cooked but still crisp. Drain and run them under cold water.

In the meantime, arrange the washed lettuce hearts, putting half on each plate. Chop the tomatoes and throw away the pips. Put them on the lettuce. Cut the peeled shallot into rings.

Put the French beans on to the plates. Cut the warm mackerel fillets into chunks and arrange on the salad with the shallot rings and olives.

Squeeze lemon juice over it all and sprinkle with olive oil.
Season lightly.

WARM SCALLOP SALAD WITH LIME

(serves 4)

Like all shellfish, scallops do contain cholesterol, but the amounts are so small and the other benefits so great that I have decided to include this lovely salad.

10 scallops
1 tblsp lemon juice
4 handfuls of mixed salad leaves, e.g. curly endive,
lettuce, red lettuce, mescalin . . .
French dressing made with lime juice (see p. 188)
fresh chives and parsley, chopped
1 lime, sliced, for garnishing

Wash the scallops carefully, remove the coral and slice the white part into three.

Wash the salad and shake dry. Dress it in vinaigrette (French dressing) made with fresh lime juice and a nut oil, walnut or hazelnut, if you have it, and arrange it on four plates.

Put the scallops into a small pan with water and lemon juice to barely cover. Bring this to the boil and allow to simmer for less than a minute. Drain and put them on to the salads. Season lightly and garnish with slices of lime.

GREEK SALAD

I'm certain that you know how to make a Greek salad – but in case you're in any doubt, it's made with small chunks of feta cheese, shiny black olives, cucumber (chunks again), torn lettuce leaves, tomato wedges and a few onion rings.

Dressing for Greek Salad
juice of 3 lemons
3 tblsp Greek honey
2 tsp sea salt
plenty of freshly ground black pepper
600 ml/1 pint Greek olive oil
½ tsp rigani (wild oregano) or fresh basil leaves, torn

Shake all ingredients together in a large screwtop jar. Taste for and adjust seasoning and sweetness. In my opinion a lot of people use too much salt – so please don't, because you can't take it out, although you can always add more on your plate.

This makes enough for many salads. It will keep for weeks in a tightly closed jar in the refrigerator. If you do not want to make so much just cut down the quantities.

CHICKEN, CELERY AND HAZELNUT SALAD

(serves 8)

1 2 kg/4½ lb chicken, with giblets
2 tblsp sunflower oil
3 tarragon sprigs
300 ml/½ pint water
4 pieces of endive (chicory)
100 g/4 oz hazelnuts, coarsely chopped
100 g/4 oz black grapes, halved and deseeded
2 tblsp chopped parsley
300 ml/½ pint French dressing (see p. 188)
sea salt and freshly ground black pepper
watercress and lettuce hearts for garnish

Remove the giblets and brush the chicken with oil. Sprinkle the chopped tarragon leaves over and place in a roasting tin. Surround with the giblets and pour in the water. Cover the tin loosely with greaseproof paper or foil and cook in a moderately hot oven (200°C, Gas Mark 6, 400°F) for 1–1¼ hours. Allow to cool.

Remove the skin and take all the chicken meat from the bone and cut it into bite-sized pieces. Combine with the endive, hazelnuts, grapes and parsley. Toss the salad in enough French dressing to moisten; season to taste.

Pile on to a serving dish and surround with small bunches of watercress and lettuce hearts.

FARMGATE SALAD

(serves 1)

Morag O'Brien runs a lovely restaurant in Midleton, Co. Cork, and this is the salad I can rarely resist at lunchtime there.

1 lettuce heart
1 tblsp coleslaw
1 dessert apple, cored and sliced
1 small bunch of grapes, deseeded
1 tblsp grated low-fat Cheddar cheese
1 tomato, sliced
3 rings of green or red sweet pepper
a little chopped spring onion
1–2 tblsp French dressing (see p. 188)

The lettuce is put on the plate first, then the coleslaw, sliced apple, bunch of grapes, cheese and tomato go on the plate in little groups. Sprinkle the sweet pepper rings, vinaigrette and spring onion on top of everything.

PASTA SHELL SALAD

(serves 4)

225 g/8 oz pasta shells
3 tblsp olive oil or sunflower oil
1½ tsp cider vinegar
sea salt and freshly ground pepper
2 oranges, peel and pith removed
1 banana, skinned and sliced
1 green pepper, deseeded and finely chopped
300 ml/½ pint low-fat yogurt

Garnish
1 lettuce
sprigs of watercress

Cook the pasta in boiling salted water for about 10 minutes. Drain and toss it in the oil and vinegar. Season with salt and plenty of pepper, and allow to cool. Cut the oranges lengthways into the centre to free the segments from the membrane.

Toss all the ingredients together and pile up the salad in a roomy dish. Surround with lettuce leaves and place a posy of watercress in the centre.

RICE SALAD

(serves 8)

450 g/1 lb long-grain rice
1 184 g/6½ oz can pimientos, rinsed and chopped
100 g/4 oz cooked peas
1 340 g/12 oz can sweetcorn, drained
1 tsp chopped lemon thyme
2 tblsp chopped chives
250 ml/scant ½ pint French dressing (see p. 188)

Cook the rice in boiling salted water for 10 minutes. Drain and sprinkle with cold water to separate the grains. Combine with the remaining ingredients and pour enough French dressing over to moisten. Toss well together and cool.

AVOCADO, MONKFISH AND PASTA SALAD

(serves 4)

2 avocados
juice of ½ lemon
225 g/8 oz monkfish, barely cooked in a little water
2 kiwi fruit
4 sticks celery
225 g/8 oz pasta shells, lightly cooked and drained
2 tblsp finely chopped parsley
2 tblsp snipped chives

Dressing
2 tsp Worcestershire sauce
a few drops of Tabasco
juice of ½ lemon and 1 orange
2 tsp sugar
½ tsp coriander seeds, crushed
sea salt and pepper
150 ml/¼ pint low-fat yogurt

Whisk the dressing together in a bowl. Halve, peel and dice the avocados and sprinkle them with lemon juice. Add the monkfish. Peel and slice the kiwi and dice the celery. Fold everything together with the dressing and the herbs.

Serve with a tomato salad and a tossed green salad.

●

WENDY'S SALAD

(serves 6)

1 small head Chinese leaves, finely shredded
225 g/8 oz grated carrots
marinated in juice of 1 small orange
1 lettuce, shredded
3 kabanos sausages, sliced
3 peaches
150 ml/¼ pint French dressing (see p. 188)
75 g/3 oz cashew nuts
1 bunch watercress

Assemble the Chinese leaves, carrot, lettuce and sausage slices in a large bowl. Just before serving, peel and slice the peaches and add to the salad with the French dressing and cashews. Toss together and serve garnished with bunches of watercress.

Note: Kabanos are garlicky sausages from Poland and can be bought at delicatessen counters everywhere.

NORWEGIAN HERRING SALAD
(serves 6)

3 pickled herrings or herring rollmops
100 g/4 oz cooked beetroot, diced
225 g/8 oz cooked potato, diced
1 onion, finely chopped
1 dessert apple, peeled and chopped
½ tsp caraway seeds
150 ml/¼ pint yogurt
4 tblsp mayonnaise (see p. 192)
sea salt and freshly ground black pepper

Cut the herrings into bite-sized pieces and mix with the prepared beetroot, potato, onion and apple. Fold into this the mayonnaise, yogurt and caraway seeds gently so as not to break up the herrings. Season well and chill. Serve on a bed of lettuce leaves.

RED CABBAGE SALAD WITH GOAT'S CHEESE
(serves 4)

½ kg/1 lb red cabbage
2 tblsp red wine vinegar
3 tblsp sunflower oil
sea salt and pepper
100 g/4 oz goat's cheese
4 slices of French bread, each cut into four
8 walnut halves

Wash the red cabbage and drain it. Shred it finely with a sharp knife. Toss the red cabbage in the wine vinegar and oil and season with a little salt and plenty of pepper. Put a small knob of cheese on each piece of bread and toast under the grill until the cheese is melting. Put the cabbage on to 4 plates with 4 pieces of cheese toast garnished with a couple of walnut halves.

Ten

DESSERTS

It is amazing how many exquisite desserts can be made without cream. There really is no end to the wonderful fruits that can be used as the seasons unfold; nowadays many more are imported from sunnier climates and they are all so tempting, luscious and exotic to round off a meal. The habit of finishing with fruit is particularly good for the heart because of its no-fat, high-fibre goodness with abundant vitamins and minerals and high water content.

The following chapter may give some new ideas and also help when fond memories of hot puddings on winter days come back to tempt you. Or when dreams of wicked desserts return, try an alternative recipe which won't shorten your life!

APRICOT SOUFFLÉ

(serves 4)

100 g/4 oz castor sugar
sunflower oil
225 g/8 oz dried apricots, soaked
twist of lemon peel
4 egg whites

Brush a 1 litre/2 pint soufflé dish with a little sunflower oil and dust with castor sugar. Cook the apricots in the water in which they were soaked, with the lemon peel, for 30 minutes, until tender. Drain and remove the peel. Purée the apricots in a liquidiser, or press through a sieve. Stir sugar in to taste.

Whisk the egg whites until firm, then fold gently and quickly into the apricot purée. Pour into the soufflé dish and cook in a moderately hot oven (200°C, Gas Mark 6, 400°F) for about 18 minutes. The soufflé should be firm sponge around the edge and creamy in the centre. Serve with yogurt.

For dinner parties decorate with a few mint leaves in the centre and serve with a swirl of raspberry sauce (see p. 179).

GERANIUM CREAMS
(serves 3)

225 g/8 oz curd cheese
150 ml/¼ pint yogurt
3 tblsp castor sugar
2 egg whites
scented geranium leaves
1 tblsp vanilla sugar
berryfruits in season

Blend the curd cheese, yogurt and sugar together in a liquidiser. Spoon into individual heart-shaped moulds lined with cheese-cloth, cover each with a scented geranium leaf and leave on a tray to drain overnight.

Turn out, if you like, on to a bed of freshly picked and prettily arranged geranium leaves. Sprinkle the remaining sugar over and serve with the fruit.

Note: Tiny wild strawberries, when in season, are delicious with the geranium creams. A little later in the year a dish of stewed blackberries works well too.

VIN ROSÉ JELLY
(serves 4–6)

Half fill a simple pottery or glass bowl with rosé wine jelly and, when it is just setting, suspend some jewel-bright summer fruits in it for an entrancing, cool summer dessert. Raspberries are lovely in this, as are little ripe redcurrants or strawberries and very thin slices of lemon.

25 g/1 oz gelatine
600 ml/1 pint hot water
350 g/12 oz sugar
1 bottle of vin rosé

Stir all the ingredients together over a low heat until the sugar is melted.

Pour into a bowl and add the fruits when the jelly is just setting so that they 'float' through it.

MICHAEL'S BANANA TREAT

(serves 2)

2 large oranges
1 pink grapefruit
2 tblsp sugar or honey
3 bananas

Cut small strips of peel from the orange and the grapefruit. They should be no bigger than matchsticks – a gadget called a 'zester' is useful for this, or a potato peeler will do. Simmer the peel for 2–3 minutes in a tiny saucepan with a little water while you prepare the fruit. Drain. There should be about 1 tblsp of this peel.

Squeeze the juice from the oranges and pour it into a saucepan or frying pan. Cut the peel from the grapefruit and then cut the segments out, leaving the membrane behind.

Sweeten the orange juice with the sugar or honey and bring it to the boil. Put into it the peeled, sliced bananas, the strips of peel and the grapefruit segments. Boil up briefly for just 1–2 minutes.

Serve straight away with some yogurt. Delicious!

CELESTIAL BANANAS

(serves 6)

A Creole dish.

sunflower oil
castor sugar to dust
6 bananas, peeled and halved lengthways
100 g/4 oz soft brown sugar
juice of 1 lemon
grated rind and juice of 1 orange
4 tblsp rum

Brush a shallow ovenproof dish with a little sunflower oil and dust with castor sugar. Lay the bananas in the bottom. Make a sauce by mixing together the remaining ingredients, and pour it over the bananas.

Cover loosely with foil and bake in the centre of a moderately hot oven (200°C, Gas Mark 6, 400°F) for 25 minutes. Baste once or twice during cooking.

HAZELNUT AND BANANA YOGURT

(serves 4)

4 tblsp granulated sugar
75 g/3 oz hazelnuts, chopped
900 ml/1½ pints low-fat yogurt
2 bananas
2 tsp lemon juice

Put the sugar into a heavy frying pan over a low heat and leave quite alone until it is a brown syrup. Stir the hazelnuts in and pour into an oiled roasting tin. When it has set, break into pieces, then wrap in a clean towel and break it up with a hammer. Alternatively the pieces can be put into a blender or food processor and coarsely ground.

Slice the bananas and turn them in lemon juice. Fold them into the yogurt.

Stir in the praline, keeping back some to sprinkle on the top.

Note: Stir the praline into the yogurt just before serving to keep crunchiness.

REDCURRANTS

When garden redcurrants and whitecurrants are ripe, picked and frosted in little bunches they make a very pretty garnish for ice creams, sorbets and desserts.

Lightly whip the white of an egg and dip the bunches in it before sprinkling castor sugar on them and putting them to dry for an hour or two before using. They look gorgeous on a bright green plate.

REDCURRANT WATER ICE

(serves 4)

450 ml/¾ pint water
225 g/8 oz sugar
0.5 kg/1 lb redcurrants, cooked in 150 ml/¼ pint water
juice of 1 lemon
1 egg white

Boil the water and sugar together for 6 minutes to make a syrup. Cool. Blend the redcurrants in a liquidiser, then press through a sieve.

Mix the cooled sugar syrup with the redcurrant purée and lemon juice. Pour into a freezer-proof polythene carton and freeze to the mushy stage. Remove and stir thoroughly, turning sides to centre. Fold into it the stiffly whisked egg white and freeze again, carefully covered. Scoop into a chilled glass bowl to serve.

Note: This recipe can also be made with blackcurrants.

LEMON SORBET

(serves 4)

3 lemons
175 g/6 oz castor sugar
600 ml/1 pint water
1 egg white

Pare the rinds of the lemons with a potato peeler and squeeze the juice. Bring the sugar and water gently to the boil, stirring until the sugar has completely dissolved. Now boil fast for 4 minutes. Add the lemon rinds, bring back to the boil and boil fast for a further 2 minutes. Put the pan in a bowl of cold water to cool the syrup. Add the lemon juice. Strain into a freezer-proof polythene carton and freeze to the mushy stage. Stir thoroughly, turning sides to centre. Fold into it the stiffly whisked egg white and return to the freezer. Keep covered in the freezer to retain the fresh flavour.

Sorbets make the perfect end to a rich meal, and really serve to liven up jaded palates.

Note: Lime sorbet is also very good – just substitute 3 limes for the lemons in the recipe.

GRAPES WITH MUSCAT WINE AND LEMON SORBET

(serves 6)

225 g/8 oz each black and green grapes, halved and pipped
2 tblsp castor sugar
150 ml/¼ pint Muscat wine
600 ml/1 pint lemon sorbet
lemon balm for garnish

Put green grapes into one bowl and black into another. Spoon castor sugar and wine, mixed together, over the grapes. Chill in the refrigerator.

When it is time to serve, layer grapes and sorbet in individual glasses and garnish each with a sprig of lemon balm.

HONEY RHUBARB SORBET

(serves 8)

The pale pink of thin young rhubarb stems gives this sorbet a very pretty colour, so green stalks are not suitable.

700 g/1½ lb rhubarb, washed, trimmed and cut into chunks
5 tblsp honey
grated zest and strained juice of 1 orange
150 ml/¼ pint low-fat yogurt
1 tblsp chopped stem ginger preserved in syrup (optional)
2 egg whites

Put the rhubarb into a bowl with the orange zest and juice and the honey. Cover and leave in a cool place for a few hours to draw out the rhubarb juices.

Cook this gently in a low oven in a covered dish, or over a gentle heat until quite soft. Cool.

Purée in a food processor or a blender until smooth. (Don't bother to wash up the processor or blender yet).

Freeze this to a slush. Stir sides to middle and stir the yogurt into it. Freeze to slush again – but by no means frozen solid.

For a smooth sorbet with no ice particles, give the rhubarb another whizz in your food processor or blender before folding into it the chopped stem ginger and stiffly whipped egg whites. Return to the freezer.

Home-made sorbets and ice creams are best eaten within a day or two of making. After that they become icy and lose their charm. This sorbet is best made the day before serving.

If it is very hard frozen, move it into the fridge to 'mature' before serving.

Buy shortbread – or make ginger short fingers – to have with this.

GOOSEBERRY ICE CREAM

(*serves* 6)

A delicious ice for a summer party.

225 g/8 oz gooseberries
about 100 g/4 oz castor sugar
300 ml/½ pint low-fat yogurt
1 egg white
mint sprigs to decorate

Purée the gooseberries briefly in a blender then rub the fruit through a sieve. Fold in the sugar to taste, and stir well. Mix in the yogurt.

Freeze in a covered freezer container. When the mixture is beginning to set to a mush, add the stiffly whisked egg white. Before the sorbet is firm, turn sides to centre and mix gently. Freeze until firm. Decorate each portion with a tiny mint sprig to serve.

REAL VANILLA ICE CREAM

If vanilla pods are hard to get for this ice cream, be sure that the essence you use is true vanilla essence and not artificial and synthetic.

450 ml/¾ pint milk
1 vanilla pod
75 g/3 oz castor sugar
2 egg yolks
1 tsp cornflour
300 ml/½ pint yogurt

Bring the milk to boiling point with the vanilla pod in it. Put this aside for the vanilla to infuse and flavour the milk. Then take out the pod and wash and dry it for using again.

Cream the egg yolks with the sugar until they are pale and fluffy. Slake the cornflour with a little cold milk and mix it to a smooth paste.

Put the vanilla-flavoured milk in a saucepan or bowl over a pan of simmering water and reheat the milk, whisking in the egg yolk, sugar and cornflour. Cook, stirring, over the boiling water until the egg yolks thicken and the custard coats the back of the wooden spoon.

Strain into a container for freezing and set aside to cool. Stir occasionally to prevent a skin forming.

When it is cold, beat the yogurt into it and set the mixture to freeze, covered. Beat and turn sides to middle several times before it is frozen.

Mature in the fridge for 25–30 minutes before serving.

SPICY RHUBARB CRUMBLE

(serves 6)

700 g/1½ lb rhubarb, cut into 2.5 cm/1 inch pieces
grated rind and juice of 1 orange
175 g/6 oz light soft brown sugar

Topping
75 g/3 oz butter
75 g/3 oz demerara sugar
175 g/6 oz digestive biscuits,
crushed with a rolling pin into crumbs
1 scant tsp ground cinnamon
1 tblsp chopped stem ginger

Lay the rhubarb in an ovenproof dish with the grated orange rind, juice and sugar. Cover with greaseproof paper or foil and bake in a moderate oven (180°C, Gas Mark 5, 350°F) for 25 to 30 minutes until the rhubarb is soft but not breaking up.

Melt the butter in a saucepan, stir into it the demerara sugar and the crumbs and spices. Cook for five minutes, stirring from time to time. Then cover the cooled, cooked rhubarb with this fudge-crumb mixture and bake in a moderately hot oven (200°C, Gas Mark 6, 400°F) for 15 to 20 minutes.

Take out of the oven and serve with yogurt.

COMPÔTE OF RHUBARB

(serves 6)

1 kg/2 lb rhubarb, washed and trimmed
100 g/4 oz light soft brown sugar
2 sugar cubes
2 oranges

Cut the rhubarb into 5 cm/2 inch lengths. Put into an enamelled or stainless steel pan with the sugar. Wash and dry the oranges, and rub the sugar cubes all over their skins to become impregnated with the orange zest. Toss these cubes in with the rhubarb.

Add the strained juice of the oranges.

Cook the fruit gently until it is soft but not disintegrating.

Serve with a bowl of yogurt and dark soft brown sugar.

SPICED PLUM COMPÔTE

(serves 4–6)

450 g/1 lb fresh plums
1 vanilla pod
1 small piece cinnamon stick
150 ml/¼ pint hot water
4 tblsp dark soft brown sugar
2 tsp cornflour

Preheat oven to 160°C, Gas Mark 3, 325°F.

Put the plums, sugar, water, vanilla and cinnamon into a thick, ovenproof dish and cover them with a lid. Cook in the oven for about 45 minutes. The plums should be tender, but not disintegrating.

When they are done, remove the plums to a serving dish with a slotted spoon. Pour the juices into a small pan and take out the vanilla and cinnamon. Bring these juices to a simmer. Mix the cornflour with 2 tblsp water until smooth, add to the juices, bring back to simmering point and cook gently until the juices have thickened slightly.

Pour this over the plums and serve warm with a bowl of yogurt.

PEACHES IN WINE

(serves 6)

150 g/5 oz castor sugar
225 ml/8 fl oz water
150 ml/5 fl oz white wine (a small wineglass)
12 peaches
juice of 1 lemon

Dissolve the sugar in the water, stirring, until it reaches boiling point. Boil for 6 minutes and then cool. Add the wine.

Meanwhile, pour boiling water over the peaches. Leave for 1 minute then plunge into cold water. Peel carefully, halve, and remove the stones. Arrange in a glass bowl and sprinkle with the lemon juice. Pour the syrup over the peaches. Cover with clingfilm and chill until required.

Serve with a pile of baby meringues.

PEARS IN RED WINE

(serves 4)

8 small cooking pears
juice of 1 lemon
175 g/6 oz sugar
150 ml/¼ pint water
1 stick cinnamon
4 cloves
3 strips lemon peel
3 strips orange peel
300 ml/½ pint red wine

Peel the pears but do not core them, and leave the stalks on. Put them in a bowl of water with the lemon juice to prevent them from discolouring.

Put the sugar and water together in a saucepan that is large enough to hold the pears. Add the cinnamon and cloves. Put in the pears, stalks upwards, and bring to the boil. Simmer for 15 minutes, covered. Add the red wine and cook, uncovered, for about 15–25 minutes, or until the pears are really tender. Test for doneness with a skewer or a pointed knife.

Stand the pears up in a glass dish. Reduce the syrup by boiling it down. Let the syrup cool a little so as not to crack the dish. Pour it over the pears.

Cover with clingfilm and put in a cool place for about 24 hours. Fish out the cinnamon, cloves and peel.

Serve with a bowl of yogurt.

Note: Make this the day before to let the pears absorb the flavours.

FLAMRI DE SEMOULE

(*serves 4*)

The flavour of the white wine is unusual in this pretty dessert, and the fresh blackcurrant sauce is truly delicious. A dinner party or family dish.

225 g/8 oz blackcurrants
castor sugar to sweeten
300 ml/½ pint white wine
3 tblsp semolina
40 g/1½ oz castor sugar
2 egg whites

Purée the blackcurrants in a liquidiser then sieve them to remove the tops and tails. Add sugar to taste.

Place the water and wine in a saucepan, bring to the boil and add the semolina. Simmer gently, stirring frequently, for about 10 minutes. Draw it off the heat and cool. Beat in the sugar. Whisk the egg whites until stiff, fold them in and pour into a lightly oiled jelly or charlotte mould. Cover and leave in the refrigerator for several hours.

Dip the base of the mould into very hot water, then turn out the flamri on a serving plate. Pour the sauce over it and serve with more sauce and a bowl of yogurt, if liked.

Note: Other soft fruits, such as raspberries, redcurrants or strawberries, can be used for the sauce.

ORANGES WITH PRALINE

(serves 8)

8 large oranges
150 g/5 oz granulated sugar
175 g/6 oz peanuts, grilled and skinned

Peel the oranges entirely free of pith with a sharp knife. Slice and arrange in a glass serving dish.

Dissolve the sugar very slowly in a frying pan over a low heat and leave until it is a brown syrup. (Don't stir, just keep your nerve.) Add the chopped peanuts and stir for two minutes. Pour into a well-oiled roasting tin and leave to set. When set hard, remove the praline from the tin, wrap in a clean cloth and break up with a hammer. Sprinkle pieces over the marinated oranges just before serving.

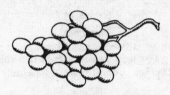

SUMMER PUDDING

(serves 8)

medium-sliced white bread
225 g/8 oz redcurrants
100 g/4 oz castor sugar
450 g/1 lb raspberries
225 g/8 oz black cherries, pitted
(or any combination of fruits)

Sauce
100–175 g/4–6 oz redcurrants and/or raspberries
50 g/2 oz castor sugar

Place a disc of greaseproof paper in the base of a large pudding bowl. Cut the crusts off the bread and line the bottom and sides of the bowl with bread slices.

Top and tail the redcurrants and place in a pan with the sugar. Heat through gently until the sugar has melted and the fruit starts to run. Add the raspberries. Bring to the boil, remove from the heat and set aside to cool. Add the cherries.

Spoon this into the bread-lined bowl. Cover with a lid of bread. Place on the top a saucer or plate that is just smaller than the bowl. Weight with something convenient (like a tin of tomatoes) and leave in the fridge overnight.

Put the fruit for the sauce into a blender with the sugar and switch on briefly. Put this through a sieve and store in a screwtop jar until you are ready to turn out the summer pudding for serving.

Turn out the summer pudding with care on to a good, roomy dish. Throw away the disc of greaseproof paper.

Pour the redcurrant and raspberry sauce over and surround the rim of the dish with raspberry leaves.

Serve with lightly whipped yogurt.

APPLE AND HAZELNUT VACHERIN

(*serves 6*)

Meringue
3 (size 2) egg whites
175 g/6 oz light golden soft brown sugar
75 g/3 oz ground roasted hazelnuts

Filling
6 tblsp fromage frais
8 tblsp apple purée, lightly sweetened
25 g/1 oz chopped roasted hazelnuts

Place silicone paper on baking sheets. Preheat the oven to 130°C, Gas Mark ½, 250°F.

Whisk the egg whites until stiff, add 2 tblsp of the sugar and continue to whisk until thick and glossy. Fold into it the remaining sugar and finally the ground hazelnuts.

Mark six 10cm/4 inch circles on the silicone paper and spoon or pipe the meringue mixture on to the paper to form nest shapes.

Bake in the preheated oven for 1½ hours, turning the baking sheets half way through cooking. Allow to cool before removing the paper.

Put the meringues on a big serving dish.

Fill the nests with a spoonful of fromage frais in the bottom and apple purée on top. Put a teaspoon of chopped hazelnuts on the top of that and serve after about an hour. This timing ensures that the meringue is soft and tender but not soggy.

POMMES ST EMILION

Whenever it says 'St Emilion' it means 'with macaroons'.

For each person, peel and core a Bramley Seedling apple.

Mix crumbled macaroons with any nice jam such as raspberry or strawberry and pack this into the hollow.

Put 2 tsp honey on the top.

For 6 apples, pour 2 tblsp water mixed with 2 tblsp rum into a shallow dish or baking tin. It should be just large enough to pack the apples in side by side. Cover with foil. Bake in a moderate oven, 180°C, Gas Mark 3, 350°F, for 25 minutes.

Uncover and baste with the syrup in the tin. Continue to bake until the apples are soft and fluffy and on the point of collapsing.

Serve with a bowl of yogurt or with vanilla ice cream (see p. 174).

FAMILY APPLE PIE

Peel, core and slice 900 g/2 lb apples and put into a buttered pie dish. Add half a cup of sugar, half a cup of sultanas and some ground spice mixed with cinnamon, nutmeg and cloves. Cover with 250 g/½ lb pastry and bake in a preheated oven (190°C, Gas Mark 5, 375°F) for 40 minutes.

FARMHOUSE RICE PUDDING

This simple and lovely recipe comes from Dorothy Hartley's *Food In England*.

'Use a very slow oven. Wash the rice. Butter the dish, cover the bottom a quarter of an inch [0.75 cm] thick in rice, and cover with three to four inches [7.5–10 cm] of sweetened milk, put some slow flavouring into it, such as a vanilla pod or a cinnamon stick, cover closely and bake, stirring often at first, till the rice has swollen and the milk is thick. If the milk is creamy – that's all. If the milk is not creamy, add a small spoonful of fine oatmeal. Raisins may be put in.'

NECTARINE TART

Filling
50 g/2 oz butter
75 g/3 oz soft brown sugar
100 g/4 oz ground almonds
1 beaten egg
3–4 nectarines

Make shortcrust pastry (see p. 205) and line an 8 inch pie tin. Bake it 'blind' for 15 minutes.

Beat all the ingredients (except the nectarines) together in a bowl. Spread this mixture over the surface of the pastry. Slice nectarines and arrange them on top, skin side up. Sprinkle with a little castor sugar and bake at 180°C, Gas Mark 4, 350°F for about 25 minutes.

Note: This tart is equally delicious with rhubarb, strawberries, peaches, raspberries, plums, pears and other fruits.

FRUIT PAVLOVA

(serves 4–6)

This recipe is from New Zealand.

3 egg whites
¼ tsp sea salt
175 g/6 oz sugar
1 tsp cornflour
1 tsp vinegar
300 ml/½ pint low-fat yogurt or fromage frais
1 kiwi fruit, peeled and sliced
6 strawberries, sliced
1 banana, sliced
6 black grapes
6 white grapes

Line a 20 cm/8 inch flan ring with well-oiled greaseproof paper. Whisk the egg whites with salt until stiff. Beat in half the sugar. Add the cornflour to the remaining sugar and fold it into the egg whites with a metal spoon. Now fold in the vinegar. Spread the mixture in the flan ring in a circle and hollow the middle slightly.

Bake for 2 hours at 120°C, Gas Mark ½, 250°F. Cool the meringue and turn it out on to a serving dish, peeling off the paper carefully. Smooth the yogurt on top. Arrange the fruit on the yogurt.

CLEMENTINE PANCAKES

(serves 4)

8 cooked pancakes (see p. 75)

Sauce
2 clementines, shredded, pips discarded
½ lemon, shredded, pips discarded
75 g/3 oz castor sugar
1 tblsp water
2 tsp cornflour
2 tblsp orange liqueur

Simmer the clementines, lemon, sugar and water in a covered pan for about 30 minutes, stirring occasionally. Do not allow the fruit to stick; add a little more water if necessary. Just before serving, moisten the cornflour with a little cold water and stir in enough to thicken the sauce slightly. Finally add the liqueur and heat through. Serve it in a sauce boat to pour over the hot pancakes.

RICH AND LIGHT CHRISTMAS PUDDING

(makes 2 puddings each to serve 6)

225 g/½ lb currants
225 g/½ lb sultanas
225 g/½ lb raisins
50 g/2 oz chopped mixed peel
225 g/8 oz butter
225 g/½ lb dark soft brown sugar
75 g/3 oz self-raising flour, sifted
1 tsp mixed spice
1 tsp grated nutmeg
225 g/½ lb fresh brown breadcrumbs
rind and juice of ½ lemon
3 eggs
75 ml/⅛ pint rum or brandy
2 tblsp black treacle
150 ml/¼ pint Guinness

Well oil two 1 litre/2 pint pudding basins and put a disc of oiled greaseproof paper in the base of each, to help the puddings turn out easily when served.

Wash and dry the fruit. Place in a large bowl with the chopped peel. Cream the butter and sugar together until light and fluffy and mix into the dried fruits. Stir in the flour, mixed spice, nutmeg and breadcrumbs. Add the grated lemon rind and strained juice. In a smaller bowl, beat together the eggs, rum or brandy and treacle. Add the Guinness and then gradually combine with the fruit mixture.

Divide this mixture between the basins and cover each with greaseproof paper or foil (making a centre fold to allow for expansion). Tuck over the outside rim and secure with string. Allow to stand in a cool place overnight.

Steam the puddings individually, in the top of a double boiler, for at least 6 hours. Cover with fresh tops and store in a cool place.

When required to serve, steam again for 2–3 hours. Turn out and top with a sprig of holly. Prick with a fork. Flame with warm rum or brandy and serve with plenty of brandy butter.

Ideally, make the puddings well in advance of Christmas, and store for a few weeks to allow the flavours to mature.

APPLE CREAM WITH ALMONDS

(*serves* 6)

700 g/1½ lb dessert apples, peeled, cored and sliced
twist of lemon peel
300 ml/½ pint low-fat yogurt
2–3 tblsp sugar
3 drops almond essence
12 roasted almonds, chopped
1 red-skinned dessert apple, cored and sliced
1 tblsp lemon juice

Poach the apples in as little water as possible, with the twist of lemon peel. Beat in the sugar, yogurt and almond essence.

Spoon into glass dishes and serve with the chopped almonds and apple slices, tossed in lemon juice, on the top.

PINEAPPLE WITH BLACK GRAPES

Peel and cut the pineapple into thick rounds. Drizzle with runny honey. Pile halved black grapes on the top and a few on the side. (Take out pips if you have time.) This is lovely with a spoonful of liqueur on the top, but it is by no means essential.

TREACLE TART

(serves 6)

225 g/½ lb shortcrust pastry (see p. 205)
4 large tblsp golden syrup
juice and rind of 1 lemon
3 tblsp fine white breadcrumbs

Roll out the pastry and line a shallow tin or pie plate, scalloping the edges. Cut ½ inch wide strips of pastry for decoration. Put the pastry in the refrigerator. Gently warm the syrup to a pouring consistency. Stir in the lemon juice, rind and the breadcrumbs. Pour all this into the pastry case, dampening it round the edge with a moist pastry brush. Twist the strips of pastry like barley sugar and lay criss-cross across the tart, pressing securely into the scalloped edge. Chill for an hour in the refrigerator and bake at 200°C, Gas Mark 6, 400°F for 35 minutes.

APRICOT MOUSSE

(serves 4)

225 g/8 oz dried apricots
50 g/2 oz sugar
1 packet lemon or orange jelly
300 ml/½ pint low-fat yogurt
2 egg whites, whipped

Soak the apricots overnight in 600 ml/1 pint water. Cook them in this water in a covered pan with the sugar. Drain off the juice and reserve. Liquidise the apricots in a blender and cool.

Dissolve the jelly in the reserved juice, which should measure about 300 ml/½ pint, and cool to setting point. Beat the barely setting jelly into the apricot purée and fold into it the yogurt and egg whites, whipped to a stiff snow. Chill in a serving bowl until set.

PEACH SUMMER CREAM

(serves 6–8)

This light and delicious pudding can also be made with strawberries, raspberries, apricots or kiwis. Sometimes I combine two fruits like strawberries and kiwi fruits, or redcurrants and peaches.

6–8 ripe peaches
600 ml/1 pint yogurt
2 tblsp soft brown sugar

Slice the peaches into a bowl or shallow dish. Pour the yogurt over the peaches and fold in gently.

Sprinkle soft brown sugar on the surface. Cover and put into the fridge for a few hours before serving.

The sugar will melt into beautiful dark brown pools on the creamy surface.

CARRAGEEN MOSS PUDDING

Carrageen moss is a type of seaweed, which is a valuable source of mineral traces.

(serves 4–6)

7 g/¼ oz cleaned, well dried carrageen
925 ml/1½ pints milk
1 tblsp sugar
1 egg
2 drops vanilla essence or 1 vanilla pod

Soak the carrageen in tepid water for 10 minutes. Remove and put in a saucepan with milk and vanilla essence or pod.

Bring to the boil and simmer very gently for 20 minutes. Pour through a strainer into a mixing bowl. The carrageen will now be swollen and exuding jelly. Rub all this jelly through the strainer and beat it into the milk with the sugar, egg yolk and vanilla essence or pod. When slightly set whisk the egg white stiffly and fold it in gently. It will rise to make a fluffy top. Serve chilled, with a fruit compôte, caramel sauce or Irish coffee sauce.

Caramel sauce
225 g/8 oz sugar
330 ml/11 fl oz hot water

Dissolve sugar in ⅓ cup of water over heat and continue cooking to a caramel. Remove from heat. Pour in the rest of the water and continue cooking until caramel is dissolved and smooth. Do not stir.

Irish coffee sauce
225 g/8 oz sugar
80 ml/3 fl oz water
250 ml/8 fl oz coffee
1 tblsp Irish whiskey

Make a caramel as above. Add coffee (made to drinking strength) instead of water. Cool, and add whiskey.

SWEET DESSERT PANCAKES
(For basic pancake batter see p. 75)

Of course pancakes can be eaten just as they are, with a dredge of sugar or a drizzle of honey and a good wedge of lemon for squeezing. Delicious, especially when they are hot from the pan.

In summer I love to fill pancakes with strawberries in sugar and lemon and perhaps with ¼ tsp grated cinnamon in the batter. Put in plenty of strawberries and fold the pancake over – the filling should be spilling out like in a cornucopia.

Pitted cherries in sugar make another wonderful filling. This time flavour the batter with kirsch, dust lightly with sugar and heat briefly in the oven. Serve on their own, or with yogurt or a little fromage frais.

Try other fillings like bananas with rum, pineapple with honey and nuts, apricots, stewed dried apricots with a scoop of low-fat ice cream. They are all good – you can dream up your own flavour.

Eleven

SAUCES AND DIPS

I have made serving suggestions for all the sauces, but doubtless you will soon discover your own favourite combinations. Many of the savoury sauces make excellent dips for raw vegetables.

BASIC FRENCH DRESSING

Oil dressings are best with leafy salads such as lettuce or young spinach leaves. They should be flavoured with a little mustard or with chopped fresh herbs and a small crushed clove of garlic.

¼ cup lemon juice or cider vinegar
1 tsp made mustard (Meaux whole-grain is good)
2 tsp runny honey
sea salt and black pepper to taste
2 tblsp chopped fresh herbs such as parsley,
lemon balm, chives, chervil, mint, fennel
1 small clove garlic, crushed
1 cup of good oil; either sunflower or olive oil

Combine all these ingredients together in a screwtop jar or a blender, giving them a good vigorous shake or whizz just before using. Taste. Use just enough to coat the salad well so that it glistens with its dressing, but not so much that the dressing lies in the bottom of the bowl.

YOGURT SALAD DRESSING

150 ml/¼ pint low-fat yogurt
2 tsp tomato ketchup (or 1 tsp tomato purée)
2 tblsp freshly chopped chives
sea salt and black pepper
2 tsp vinegar
½ tsp Worcestershire sauce

Stir all the ingredients together in the order listed and taste for the exact effect you want. (Always taste as you go when cooking.)

This is delicious and a little unusual; it goes particularly well on avocado pear or salad with avocado in it.

LOW-CHOLESTEROL 'SOURED CREAM'

(makes 150 ml/¼ pint)

2 tblsp skimmed milk
1 tblsp lemon juice
225 g/8 oz low-fat quark or fromage frais
sea salt to taste

Measure the ingredients into a liquidiser in the order listed above. Cover and blend for 30 seconds or until smooth. Chill.

Snipped chives are excellent stirred into this, to accompany meat or fish, or to top a baked jacket potato. Serve as a dressing for salad, or as a sauce for a mousse with the addition of some freshly chopped tarragon or dill. If using in a hot dish, add at the last moment.

NELL'S SALAD DIP

¼ tsp caraway seeds
¼ tsp celery salt
150 ml/¼ pint low-fat yogurt

Put the caraway seeds, celery salt and yogurt into a small screw-top jar. Stir them together and screw on the lid tightly.

It couldn't be much simpler. It can be varied by using other spices such as a few crushed coriander seeds or a little tomato ketchup and Worcestershire sauce.

Note: Try yogurt salad dressing (see p. 189) and cucumber sauce (see p. 193) as dips too.

AVOCADO DIP

2 avocados
2 tblsp lemon juice
2 tblsp olive oil
1 clove garlic, crushed
1 tblsp chopped chives or green spring onion tops
sea salt
4 drops Tabasco
black pepper

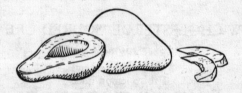

Peel, stone and chop the avocados into the bowl. Add the rest of the ingredients and blend until smooth. Taste for seasoning. Serve with chunks of raw vegetable such as carrot, cauliflower, radish, celery and strips of sweet red and green pepper, or those lovely tortilla corn chips.

PEANUT SAUCE

Peanuts are not actually nuts at all, but 'legumes'. They are rich in monounsaturated oil. This, when balanced with polyunsaturates, is beneficial to the heart.

Peanut sauce makes a lovely dip for raw vegetables such as strips of sweet pepper, chunks of cucumber, florets of cauliflower, strips of carrot and celery, young turnips, radishes and chicory leaves.

It also makes a good vegetarian meal when served on a dish of savoury brown rice and accompanied by a salad.

2 cloves garlic, crushed
2 tblsp sunflower oil
1 tsp coriander seeds, crushed
2.5 cm/1 inch cube of fresh ginger (about the size of a walnut)
2 tblsp tamari *or* soy sauce
juice of 1 lemon
2 tsp honey
sea salt and black pepper
175 g/6 oz ground peanuts
¼ tsp dried chilli flakes (optional:
skip these if you have young children)

Gently fry the garlic in oil with the crushed coriander. Chop the ginger finely and if you have used a garlic crush, push it through this. Add the ginger to the pan.

Stir in tamari, lemon juice, honey, seasoning to taste, peanuts and chilli flakes. Add enough hot water (about 150 ml/¼ pint) to make the sauce to the right consistency. Simmer for a few minutes and check the flavour again before serving.

DILL SAUCE

(makes about 300 ml/½ pint)

It is well worth planting a packet of dill seeds in your garden every year to grow this delicious herb which the Scandinavians love so. It is a pretty feathery plant which looks very much like fennel but has a totally different flavour. Use it in salads, on potatoes, with fish and in a velouté sauce for boiled leg of lamb.

The following sauce is excellent with pickled or marinated herring. Soak the herring fillets first if they are too strong.

150 ml/¼ pint low-fat yogurt
150 ml/¼ pint fromage frais
1 tsp Dijon mustard
4 tblsp freshly chopped dill
sea salt and freshly ground pepper

Mix all the ingredients together and taste for seasoning.

MAYONNAISE

(makes generous 300 ml/½ pint)

1 egg
½ tsp dry mustard
¼ tsp sea salt
3 tsp sugar
1 tblsp lemon juice
300 ml/½ pint olive oil

Break the egg into the goblet of a liquidiser. Add mustard, salt, sugar and lemon juice. Turn on at low speed and add half the oil in a very small stream through the 'feed', stopping every few seconds to let the egg take up and emulsify the oil. The remaining oil can be poured in quite steadily.

Home-made mayonnaise can also be made with vinegar and sweetened with a little honey. It can be flavoured with the addition of finely chopped chives, parsley, fresh herbs, garlic, capers, olives or gherkins.

PESTO

1 bunch fresh basil
50 g/2 oz shelled walnuts
25 g/1 oz Parmesan cheese
1 clove garlic, crushed
1 tblsp lemon juice
4 tblsp olive oil
black pepper

Strip the basil leaves off the stalks and put the leaves into a food processor with the other ingredients. Process briefly and turn into a bowl. This is a classic sauce to serve with pasta.

SAUCE TARTARE

(makes just under 450 ml/¾ pint)

2 tblsp mayonnaise
juice of ½ lemon
450 ml/¾ pint low-fat yogurt
1 tsp Worcestershire sauce
4 drops Tabasco sauce
sea salt and black pepper
1 tblsp chopped capers
1 tblsp freshly chopped chives
1 tblsp chopped gherkin or dill pickle

Stir and combine all the ingredients together, and allow to stand for a few hours in the refrigerator before serving. Sauce tartare is traditionally served with fish.

HORSERADISH AND WALNUT SAUCE

(makes 450 ml/¾ pint)

Excellent with cold beef, or smoked trout or mackerel.

2 tblsp freshly grated horseradish
grated rind of ½ lemon and 2 tsp juice
75 g/3 oz walnuts, chopped
150 ml/¼ pint low-fat yogurt
100 g/4 oz fromage frais
1 tsp sugar
sea salt and freshly ground white pepper

Combine all the ingredients together. Serve in a sauce boat.

CUCUMBER SAUCE

Excellent with mackerel or cold salmon.

½ cucumber, peeled, deseeded and chopped
sea salt
225 g/8 oz fromage frais
2 tblsp low-fat yogurt
2 tblsp chopped dill or mint
white pepper

Salt the cucumber lightly and drain in a colander for 15 minutes. Blend cucumber and fromage frais in a liquidiser with enough yogurt to bring the sauce to the consistency of thick cream. Stir in the dill or mint and season to taste.

CRANBERRY SAUCE

(*serves 6*)

175 g/6 oz cranberries
2 tblsp water
2 tblsp vanilla sugar
a little grated orange rind
2 tblsp port

Place all the ingredients in a saucepan. Cook over a gentle heat, stirring, until the cranberries pop and burst. Serve hot, in a sauce boat, to accompany roast turkey.

BREAD SAUCE

This is wonderful, the perfect accompaniment to roast turkey. Grate 50 g/2 oz of onion and simmer in half a pint of milk, adding 40 g/1½ oz butter, sea salt and white pepper. This can be done the day before.

Shortly before you need the sauce, add 50–75 g/2–3 oz white breadcrumbs and a clove. Simmer for a few minutes.

ONION SAUCE

This is an ideal sauce to serve with lamb or pork, or vegetable dishes such as marrow or stuffed vegetables. Good with turkey and chicken too.

3 large Spanish onions, chopped or sliced
2 tblsp sunflower oil
1 large cooking apple, peeled and chopped
2 cloves
2 tblsp vermouth
½ tblsp sea salt
lots of white pepper, ground
300 ml/½ pint low-fat yogurt

Sauté the onions gently in oil in a covered pan, without browning them, with the apple. Add the cloves, vermouth, salt, pepper and yogurt. Simmer for about 10 minutes. Remove the cloves and serve hot.

WHITE SAUCE

(makes 600 ml/1 pint)

600 ml/1 pint skimmed milk
½ small onion, peeled and sliced
3 parsley stalks
1 small bay leaf
1 blade of mace
6 peppercorns
75 g/3 oz butter
3½ level tblsp flour
sea salt and pepper

Season the milk by bringing it to the boil in a saucepan with the onion, parsley, bay leaf, mace and peppercorns. Simmer for a minute and then set aside to infuse for half an hour.

Melt the butter in a saucepan, remove from the heat and stir in the flour. Return to the heat and let it bubble for another minute, stirring. It will be a pale creamy colour.

Strain the milk and stir it in, about a quarter at a time, bringing each addition to the boil and blending it in completely before adding any more. Simmer for five minutes.

Taste and season carefully.

Keep this sauce warm over boiling water or, alternatively, allow it to cool. Prevent a skin from forming by pouring a little melted butter over the surface. (Another trick is to lay a piece of clingfilm on the surface.)

TOMATO SAUCE

2 onions, peeled and chopped
2 cloves garlic, crushed
3 tblsp olive oil
1 red and 1 green pepper
450 g/1 lb ripe tomatoes, peeled, deseeded and roughly chopped
½ tsp sugar
3 tblsp red wine
sea salt and black pepper

Melt the onions and garlic in olive oil over a gentle heat.

Blanch the peppers in boiling water for about three minutes. Remove all the pips and the pith and cut the flesh into strips.

Add this to onion, along with the tomatoes, sugar, red wine and seasoning.

Simmer slowly until the sauce thickens.

There are endless variations and additions to this to suit your taste. Here are some:

Add a coarsely grated carrot to the onion and garlic, or add herbs such as oregano (just a pinch) or a little chopped fresh rosemary. I sometimes throw in a little twist of orange or lemon peel, a few finely chopped mushrooms or a hot chilli pepper (again, add to the onion at the start), and a teaspoon of tomato purée will enrich the sauce if the tomatoes lack flavour.

Serve with vegetables, pasta, rice, eggs, fish, chicken or egg dishes.

VELOUTÉ SAUCE

(makes 600ml/1 pint)

50g/2oz butter
40g/1½oz flour
600ml/1 pint chicken or veal stock
a strip of lemon peel
sea salt and white pepper

Melt the butter and stir in the flour to form the roux. Heat the stock to boiling and add to the roux a little at a time, stirring vigorously with a wooden spoon or whisk. The sauce should cook for at least 6–7 minutes with the strip of lemon peel, be stirred constantly, and become the thickness of runny cream. Season to taste and strain through a sieve before serving.

Note: Fish velouté is made in the same way, using fish stock.

SPICED PEACH SAUCE

1 large tin peach slices
3 tblsp vinegar
1 tblsp soft brown sugar
4 cloves
1 stick cinnamon
1 tblsp finely chopped shallots
2 tsp crushed black peppercorns

Drain the juice from the peaches into a saucepan and set aside the peach slices. Add everything else to the juice and simmer for 10 minutes. Pour this over the peaches. Leave to stand for at least a day for the flavour to mature.

Serve hot with grilled ham or chicken, duck or pork.

A LAST-MINUTE RED PEPPER SAUCE

4–6 tblsp olive oil
1 clove garlic, crushed
¼ tsp oregano
1 tin sweet red peppers, drained, rinsed and finely chopped
seasoning

Simmer all together for 5 minutes or so.

If you have the time and the inclination, add 1 tsp tomato purée and 1 glass red wine and allow the sauce to bubble for another few minutes.

MUSHROOM SAUCE

(*makes about 600 ml/1 pint*)

This is a good accompaniment for fish, chicken and veal dishes.

1 small onion, peeled and chopped
3 tblsp sunflower oil
450 g/1 lb button mushrooms, wiped and sliced
juice of ½ lemon
2 tblsp flour
300 ml/½ pint dry cider or white wine
sea salt and pepper
3 tblsp fromage frais

Soften the onion in the oil and add the mushrooms and lemon juice. Shake the flour over and stir in for a minute or two. Gradually add the cider or wine, stirring all the time, and bring to the boil. Season with salt and pepper. Simmer for a few minutes and stir in the fromage frais before serving.

APPLE SAUCE WITH CALVADOS

This is lovely as a sauce with pork, duck or goose, and it makes a delicious pudding with meringues or with yogurt folded into it. Try it too, with the addition of a few sultanas, as a filling for pancakes.

> 1 kg/2 lb dessert apples
> ¼ tsp grated nutmeg
> ¼ tsp ground cinnamon
> 1 tblsp runny honey
> calvados to taste

Peel and core the apples and slice them thinly into a casserole. Add the spices and honey with a tablespoon of water. Cover the casserole and put in a preheated oven at 190°C, Gas Mark 5, 375°F for about 40 minutes. Stir occasionally.

Take out of the oven, then put the apple sauce into a blender and add a few tablespoons of calvados – an orange liqueur will do if you prefer, but the calvados is best!

ANCHOVY SAUCE

(makes about 250 ml/8 fl oz)

Lovely as a dip with young, raw vegetables.

1 56 g/2 oz can anchovy fillets, soaked in milk
150 g/5 oz fromage frais
2 tsp lemon juice
5 drops Tabasco sauce (optional)
3 tblsp low-fat yogurt
1 tblsp chopped chives

Liquidise in a blender or food processor, or work all the ingredients except the chives, in the order listed, with a wooden spoon, until you have obtained a smooth sauce. Fold in the chives. Set aside for the flavours to mature for a few hours before serving.

MUSTARD SAUCE

(makes about 300ml/½ pint)

This is excellent with all sausage, pork and ham dishes, or as an accompaniment to crudités. It is also a good sauce to serve with mackerel and herring.

2 tblsp whole-grain mustard
150ml/¼ pint low-fat yogurt
150ml/¼ pint mayonnaise
2 tsp honey

Combine all the ingredients. Turn out into a bowl or sauce boat.

FURTHER IDEAS

To dress a dish of lightly cooked cauliflower or broccoli: combine 2 tsp sweet paprika pepper with a small carton of low-fat yogurt, add seasoning to taste with a squeeze of lemon juice and warm the mixture over a gentle heat. Nothing could be easier. Dust the top with a little paprika for its beautiful colour.

To make a delicious sauce to serve with barbecued food: whisk together 1 tsp honey, 1 tsp lemon juice and two small cartons of low-fat yogurt. Stir in 1 tblsp each of chopped parsley and mint.

Orange and nut sauce is good as a filling for pancakes or as a dessert accompaniment. Stir the flesh of 1 orange, 2 tblsp chopped nuts and 4 chopped dates into a small carton of low-fat yogurt.

Twelve

BAKING

A LOAF OF BREAD

Here with a Loaf of Bread beneath the Bough,
A Flask of Wine, a Book of Verse – and Thou
Beside me singing in the Wilderness –
And Wilderness is Paradise enow.

Edward Fitzgerald, *The Rubaiyat of Omar Khayyam*

There is no greater compliment to family or friends than home-baked bread. It is interesting that the busiest people are usually the ones who bake their own. Actually it is not a time-consuming job, but it does require that one is about while the dough 'proves'. With only a little skill and imagination, it is possible always to have varied and healthy loaves at a lower cost than bought bread. It is a creative and rewarding job and extremely soothing. The fragrant smell of home-made bread is one of the delights of life, and the most simple food imaginable becomes a feast when served with a fresh crusty loaf.

I use practically no other flour than wholemeal for bread-making, to avoid having to knead the dough, and for the fibre which is good for you. Fast-action dried yeast is a blend of dried yeast and bread improvers that makes bread-baking much faster and simpler.

The basic utensils are easily obtained and inexpensive: a large bowl, which can be china, pottery, metal or plastic and should be about one foot in diameter; a cheap measuring jug is a help; spoons and scales are too, but they are not essential; I think that bread tins are essential, although you *can* use cake tins and even flower pots, but the tins are an ideal shape (try not to wash them between use – repeated oiling and use builds up a lovely dark sheen that is a better surface than non-stick); you will need a baking sheet for rolls and soda bread and plaited breads; a spatula is very useful.

Put dough to rise either in a lightly greased saucepan with a close-fitting lid, or in a lightly floured polythene bag – making sure that there is room for double the quantity. This gives protection from draughts and dryness by providing an even temperature and moisture.

If the texture of your bread is coarse with long, unsightly holes, and maybe has a 'flying top' crust too, the cause is probably under-ripeness – that is, insufficient rising. Remember always to leave bread to rise and prove until it has doubled in size.

If the texture is bleached white or greyish and dry, this is often caused by over-ripeness – meaning that the dough was allowed to rise and prove for too long, therefore weakening the dough.

Kneading the dough is easy; unlike with pastry, you're allowed to be tough. Pick up the edge of the dough and, using your knuckles, push it firmly over to the centre. Turn the dough and continue in the same way.

Fresh yeast is probably best, and dried yeast is an excellent standby, as is the fast-action one that I mentioned earlier.

STEP-BY-STEP BREAD-MAKING

(makes 4 × 450g/1lb loaves)

Making bread is really easy despite popular belief.

1.35 kg/3 lb wholemeal flour
18 g/¾ oz (a scant tblsp) salt
50 g/2 oz fresh yeast (half if using dried)
3 tsp runny honey *or* raw Barbados sugar *or* molasses
1.2 litres/2 pints tepid water *or* milk and water

Place the flour and salt in a large bowl and set it in a warm place.

Preheat the oven to 230°C, Gas Mark 8, 450°F.

Blend the yeast with the honey and about 300 ml/½ pint of the liquid and put this in a warm place too for it to froth up.

When the yeast is thoroughly active, pour it into the flour with most of the rest of the liquid. Mix with your hand to make a fairly wet dough. Put the dough on a well-floured board and knead for 5–10 minutes. Pick up the edges of the dough and, using your knuckles, push it firmly over the centre. Turn the dough and continue in the same way.

Oil 4 (450 g/1 lb) loaf tins generously and divide the dough amongst them. Cover the tins with a clean cloth or put them into a floured polythene bag and set them in a warm place to double in size.

Uncover the tins and put them into the hot oven for approximately 40–50 minutes. The loaves will be baked when they are brown and crisp on the top and sound hollow when tapped. If you want the loaves crisp all round, finish them by removing them from the tins, and replacing in the oven, about 10 minutes before the end of cooking time.

Put the bread on a wire rack to cool.

IRISH BROWN BREAD

450 g/16 oz brown flour
25 g/1 oz wheatgerm
25 g/1 oz bran
300 ml/½ pint buttermilk
25 g/1 oz sugar
25 g/1 oz oatmeal
1 egg
2 tsp sea salt
2 tsp breadsoda

Put all ingredients except egg and buttermilk into a bowl. Lightly finger it.

Beat the egg and add the buttermilk to it.

Add egg and buttermilk to ingredients and mix with fork. Do not knead.

Put in a hot oven (200°C, Gas Mark 8, 400°F) for 40 minutes.

BALLYMALOE BROWN BREAD

(makes 4 loaves)

The main ingredients of these loaves – wholemeal flour, treacle and yeast – are highly nutritious.

1.5 kg/3 lb wholemeal flour
approx 1.5 litres/2½ pints water at blood heat
(mix yeast with 300 ml/½ pint lukewarm water)
1 tblsp sea salt
1–2 well-rounded tsp black treacle
50–100 g/2–4 oz yeast
sesame seeds (optional)

(makes 1 loaf)
450 g/1 lb wholemeal flour
400–450 ml/12–15 fl oz water at blood heat
(mix yeast with approx 150 ml/5 fl oz lukewarm water)
1 tsp black treacle
1 tsp salt
25 g/1 oz yeast
sesame seeds (optional)

Mix flour with salt and warm it in the cool oven of an Aga or Esse or in the gas or electric oven when it's starting to heat up. Mix treacle with some of the water (approx 300 ml/½ pint for 4 loaves and 150 ml/5 fl oz for 1 loaf) in a small bowl, crumble the yeast and add to the treacle. Put the bowl in a warm position such as the back of the cooker. Grease bread tins and put them to warm. Also warm a clean tea-towel. Look to see if the yeast is rising. It will take approximately 5 minutes to do so and will have a creamy and slightly frothy appearance on top. Stir it well and pour it with most of the remaining water into the flour to make a wettish dough. Put the mixture into the greased, warmed tins and sprinkle with sesame seeds if you like. Put the tins back in the same position as used previously to raise the yeast. Put the tea-towel over the tins. In approximately 20 minutes the loaves will have risen to twice their original size. Now bake them in a hot oven, 230°C, Gas Mark 8, 470°F, for 45–50 minutes, or until they look nicely browned and sound hollow when tapped.

Dried yeast may be used instead of baker's yeast. Follow the same method but use only half the weight given for fresh yeast. Allow longer time for it to rise.

BARM BRACK

(makes 1 × 1 kg/2 lb loaf)

350 g/12 oz mixed dried fruit
150 ml/¼ pint tea
100 g/4 oz soft brown sugar
225 g/8 oz self-raising flour
pinch of salt
1 egg

Soak the mixed fruit in the tea with the sugar for 24 hours.

Grease and line a 1 kg/2 lb loaf tin. Sift flour and salt and add to fruit with lightly beaten egg. Mix well till blended. Turn into prepared tin. Bake in centre of moderate oven (180°C, Gas Mark 4, 350°F) for about 1½ hours or until cooked through. Turn out and cool. Store in foil or an airtight tin. Serve sliced thinly and spread lightly with butter.

This is not a true barm brack because it is not made with yeast. But we always called it barm brack as children.

THE SECRET OF PERFECT PASTRY

I used to be terrified of making pastry; it always seemed to be such tricky stuff. But in reality there are no secrets or mysteries – just a few guidelines.

Light handling is a must. The fat has to be cold and rubbed gently into the flour so that it does not become greasy. I use a pastry cutter or a food processor for this job. Go very easy with the food processor though: only pulse barely long enough to cut in the fat (so that it looks like breadcrumbs), then pour in a little less liquid than you would use by hand, and pulse for a second or two more until the pastry throws itself into a ball. Stop right there.

The amount of liquid that is used is critical. Too much and the pastry will be hard or tough; too little and it will be difficult to handle – too 'short'.

Rest the pastry for at least half an hour after making it and before rolling it out. This allows the liquid to be absorbed, making the pastry easier to handle. It also enables the gluten to relax, thereby avoiding shrinkage in the oven.

Use ice-cold water.

A pinch of salt brings out the flavour. Add a teaspoon or two of castor sugar to sweeten and add herbs or ground nuts to savoury pastry.

I enrich the pastry of our mince pies at Christmas by replacing 25 g/1 oz flour with 25 g/1 oz ground almonds in each 225 g/½ lb pastry.

When rolling out pastry, use a well-floured board, and flour the pin and the board rather than the pastry. Use short strokes in one direction. Turn the pastry around and do not let it stick. Try always to use your first rolling (even if it needs patching). Pile trimmings up for a second rolling.

Line a flan case and leave a little ledge of pastry when cutting it away. Raise this and deepen the case by pinching it up all around.

Prick the base of this case with a fork and bake 'blind' by laying on it greaseproof paper or foil, with some crusts or beans spread over. Cook like this for 15 minutes. Remove the paper/foil and beans; cook for a further 10 minutes. Now put in your chosen filling and return to the oven until the centre is puffed and set.

SHORTCRUST PASTRY

(makes 225 g/8 oz dough)

225 g/8 oz wholemeal flour, sifted
a pinch of salt
150 g/5 oz White Flora
3 tblsp cold water

Cut fat into flour as described before, or use thumb and next two fingers to rub the fat lightly into the flour.

Sprinkle 3 tblsp water on to the mixture and cut it in with a knife to incorporate. Gently bring the pastry together with your hand. Add a few drops more water if the pastry seems too dry.

Form into a reasonable ball on a floured surface. Cover with clingfilm and set aside in a cool place for half an hour.

Use as needed.

HIGH-FIBRE PASTRY

100 g/4 oz wholewheat flour
50 g/2 oz oat bran
75 g/3 oz White Flora
1–2 tblsp cold water

Mix together the flour and oat bran. Add the White Flora, in small pieces. Rub in lightly and quickly until the mixture resembles fine breadcrumbs. Add 1–2 tblsp cold water and mix to a firm dough. Wrap in clingfilm and chill for 15 minutes before using.

Note: White Flora is a good low-cholesterol shortening. It is, however, not so full of flavour as butter, but a healthy alternative for anyone on a cholesterol-lowering diet.

EASY-MIX PASTRY WITH OIL

(makes 175 g/6 oz dough)

5 tblsp pure corn oil
3 tblsp water
175 g/6 oz plain flour (*or* use self-raising flour
for a lighter, crumblier texture)
½ tsp salt

Whisk together the oil and water and pour all at once on to the sifted flour and salt. Mix with a fork, combine, then knead lightly to a manageable dough which leaves the sides of the bowl clean.

Immediately roll out thinly, between sheets of greaseproof paper, without extra flour. The easiest way to use the pastry is to peel off the top paper and place the crust in position by inverting it so that the underside paper is on top; peel paper off.

MACAROONS

175 g/6 oz ground almonds
275 g/10 oz castor sugar
3 egg whites
20 g/¾ oz cornflour
almond essence
rice paper
split almonds

Mix the ground almonds with the sugar, lightly whip the egg whites and work them in thoroughly with the almonds and sugar. Add the cornflour and almond essence to this.

When the mixture is well creamed, put it into a forcing bag equipped with a star nozzle. Spread rice paper on baking sheets and now pipe the mixture in small star-shaped blobs about 5cm/2 inches across. Decorate by pressing a small split almond into the middle of each one.

Bake in a preheated oven, 190°C, Gas Mark 5, 375°F, for about 20 minutes.

Cool and store in an airtight tin.

TUILES AMANDES

(makes about 18)

Delicate and crisp. A lovely accompaniment to fruit desserts, such as fools and sorbets.

2 egg whites
90 g/3½ oz caster sugar, sifted
¼ tsp vanilla essence
¼ tsp almond essence
25 g/1 oz almonds, shredded
50 g/2 oz butter, melted but not too hot

Whisk together the egg whites and castor sugar until thick. Fold in the sifted flour. Add the vanilla and almond essences, shredded almonds and butter and mix all carefully together.

Line 2 large baking trays with non-stick baking paper and put small spoonfuls of the mixture on each, spaced well apart (the biscuits will spread out while cooking).

Bake in a moderately hot oven (190°C, Gas Mark 5, 375°F) for about 6 minutes, until pale gold. Remove from the oven. Lift off the tuiles while still warm and curl them quickly round the barrel of a rolling pin. Cool on a wire tray and store carefully in an airtight tin.

BRANDY SNAPS

(makes about 30)

100 g/4 oz golden syrup
100 g/4 oz brown sugar
100 g/4 oz butter
2 tsp lemon juice
100 g/4 oz plain flour
¼ tsp sea salt
1 tsp ground ginger

Put the syrup, sugar and butter in a saucepan and heat, stirring, until the sugar has melted. Cool slightly and stir in the lemon juice. Sift together the flour, salt and ginger and fold into the syrup mixture.

Place small spoonfuls, well apart, on baking trays lined with non-stick paper. Cook for 8 minutes in a moderate oven (160°C, Gas Mark 3, 325°F). Allow to cool for a minute, then lift with a palette knife and shape the brandy snaps round the handle of a wooden spoon. Cool on a wire tray and store in an airtight tin.

MERINGUES

3 egg whites
175 g/6 oz castor sugar
non-stick vegetable parchment

Whisk the egg whites until stiff in a clean bowl. Add 2 tblsp castor sugar and whisk again until stiff. Fold in the remaining sugar.

Line a large baking sheet with non-stick vegetable parchment.

Use a forcing bag with a star nozzle to pipe the meringue on to the paper.

Bake in the coolest oven (110°C, Gas Mark ¼, 225°F) for about four hours or until the meringues can be easily removed from the paper with a palette knife.

Store in an airtight tin until needed.

HAZELNUT BISCUITS

(makes about 30)

175 g/6 oz hazelnuts, ground
175 g/6 oz plain flour
75 g/3 oz castor sugar
175 g/6 oz butter
whole hazelnuts to decorate

Mix all the ingredients together and knead to a dough. Put to one side in a cool place to stiffen.

Divide the dough into small equal-sized pieces and roll into balls. Press on to greased baking trays, flatten out, and place a whole hazelnut firmly on each biscuit. Bake in a moderately hot oven (190°C, Gas Mark 5, 375°F) for 10–12 minutes. Allow to cool slightly on the baking trays before transferring to a wire cooling rack.

INDEX

treacle tart, 185
vin rosé jelly, 169–70
dill sauce, 191
diplomat soup, 38
dips, *see* sauces and dips
Dover sole veronique, 91–2
duck, 121
  duck with olives, 123–4
  duckling with turnips, 122–3
  roast duck with Seville orange
    sauce and stuffing, 121–2

easy-mix pastry with oil, 206
eels, smoked, 85
eggs, 15
emerald soup, 42–3

family apple pie, 181
Farmgate salad, 164–5
farmhouse rice pudding, 181
fats, 7, 9, 10–12, 13–15, 16
fennel, braised, 150–1
fillet of turbot with stuffed braised
    lettuce leaves, 101–2
fish, 11, 20, 85–106
  fish in a brick, 92
  fish pie, 99
  fish soup, 53
  fish velouté, 196
  Mrs Muller's fish mousse, 90
  salt fish chowder, 104–5
  see also anchovies; cod; Dover
    sole; eels; grey mullet; haddock;
    hake; herrings; lemon sole;
    mackerel; monkfish; red mullet;
    salmon; sardines; smoked fish;
    trout; tuna fish; turbot
fishcakes
  salmon fishcakes, 103–4
flamri de semoule, 178
flour, 17
flummery, 33
French beans
  French beans and mushrooms
    vinaigrette, 62
  mushroom and bean salad with
    hazelnut dressing, 157
French dressing, basic, 188–9
French onion soup, 48
fresh tomato juice cocktail, 61
Friendly Hall sweet pepper soup, 40

fromage frais
  roast chicken with fromage frais
    and lemon, 109–10
fruit, 17, 21, 26
  fruit pavlova, 182–3
  see also apples; apricots; avocados;
    bananas; blackcurrants;
    cherries; clementines;
    gooseberries; grapefruit; grapes;
    kiwi fruit; lemons; limes; melon;
    nectarines; olives; oranges;
    peaches; pears; pineapple;
    plums; prunes; raspberries;
    redcurrants; rhubarb;
    strawberries

game, *see* poultry and game
garlic, 18, 148, 149
  tomato soups with garlic and
    tarragon, 44
gazpacho, 36
geranium creams, 169
ginger
  baked salmon with fresh ginger and
    spring onions, 103
globe artichokes, 152–3
gooseberries
  gooseberry ice cream, 174
  grilled mackerel with gooseberry
    sauce, 97
goulash
  Hungarian veal goulash, 146–7
grains, 17
grandmother's braised steak, 136
grapefruit
  citrus salad, 30
  hot grapefruit, 30–1
grapes
  chicken livers with grapes, 69
  grapes with muscat wine and
    lemon sorbet, 173
  pineapple with black grapes, 185
gravad lax, 88
Greek salad, 163
Greek soup, 43
green peppers
  Friendly Hall sweet pepper soup,
    40
  lamb and pepper kebabs, 132–3
  stuffed green peppers, 71
grey mullet